'CARRY YOUR BAG, SIR?'

By the same author
Golf: the history of an obsession

Co-author of
The Compleat Golfer
Golf in the making
Royal Blackheath
Shortspoon

▷ *A game at*
Wimbledon at the end
of the 19th century.
Both the boy caddies
are well dressed.

'CARRY YOUR BAG, SIR?'

A History of Golf's Caddies

DAVID STIRK

H. F. & G. Witherby Ltd

First published in Great Britain 1989 by
H. F. & G. WITHERBY LTD
14 Henrietta Street, London WC2E 8QJ

British Library Cataloguing in Publication Data
Stirk, David I.
Carry your bag, Sir? : a history of golf's caddies.
1. Golf. Caddies to 1988
I. Title
796.352

ISBN 0-85493-172-4

Designed by Roger Kohn
Typeset in Great Britain by Falcon Graphic Art Limited
Printed and bound by Biddles Ltd, Guildford and King's Lynn

CONTENTS

1. WHAT'S IN A NAME?

The term for those who carried golf clubs has been subject to a number of changes in the past, before arriving at the generally accepted 'caddie'.

Etymologically, dictionaries state that the name stems from the French word *'cadet'*, meaning the youngest son of a family, or, in military terminology, someone who enters the army as a private with the intention of becoming an officer. One suspects, however, that this is because no word has been found in the earliest English or Scottish dictionaries which resembles the word 'caddie', rather than any more positive connection.

The *Etymological English Dictionary* published by W & R Chambers in 1885 seemed a likely source of information as Robert Chambers, one of the authors, was a well known and distinguished amateur golfer. Alas, the word 'caddie' does not occur!

CAWDYS AND CADIES

According to Jamieson's *Etymological Dictionary of the Scottish Language* (1840), in 1730 a Captain Burt described people who existed in Edinburgh at that time as:
'Cawdys . . . useful Blackguards, who attend coffee houses and publick places to go on errands.' He goes on to say that they are wretches who lie in the streets in rags at night. Having given them a verbal castigation he then, surprisingly, goes on to say that: 'They are often considerably trusted, and, as I have been told, seldom or never prove unfaithful.'

◁ *William Gunn, alias 'Caddie Willie' or 'Daft Willie Gunn'. History does not relate when he was born; he carried in the early part of the 19th century at Bruntsfield. A Highlander, he did not speak good English.*

During the golfing season he lived in a garret in Edinburgh and existed entirely on baps. Every autumn, when the season closed, he tramped back to his native Highlands, reappearing the following spring. In 1820 he went back to the Highlands, as usual, but was never seen again.

He was eccentric but 'quite harmless'. His most obvious eccentricity were his clothes. As was the custom, he received clothes from the various masters for whom he carried, his peculiarity was that he wore all of them at the same time. He had three or four coats and had to cut the sleeves off the inner ones in order to get them on. He wore three pairs of trousers and three bonnets.

His other peculiarity was that he never addressed his masters by name but referred to them by profession, a surgeon he referred to as a 'man of the knife', a clergyman as a 'man of God', a gardener as a 'man of the cabbage' and so on: 'Ye'll be needin' a lang iron here, man of the knife'.

Other writers of about this time refer to them as 'cadies' and their descriptions suggest that they were itinerant messengers of all ages and particularly to be found in Edinburgh in the 18th century. They not only delivered messages but also carried parcels.

Despite sleeping rough and looking dirty, they were trustworthy and had a sketchy organisation; individuals admitted to 'the fraternity' (as it was sometimes called) had to find surety for their good behaviour, and there was a senior 'cadie', known as 'the Constable of the Cadies', who had the authority to punish delinquents with fines or, on occasion, with corporal punishment.

For more detailed information about the organisation of the Edinburgh cadies, which includes an Ordinance of the City of Edinburgh regulating the charges and the areas in which cadies might operate, the reader is referred to the excellent account given by David Hamilton in *Early Golf in Edinburgh and Leith*.

CLUBMEN

A poem about golf written in 1819 includes the statement:
'Whilst trotting clubman follows fast behind,
Prepared with ready hand and tees to lay.'

The term 'clubman' has not been found elsewhere and it may be an example of poetic licence. Perhaps the poet was not familiar with the term 'cadie' but the term 'clubman' for one who carries golf clubs seems quite reasonable and may well have been another alias.

CADS

David Robertson, a member of a famous feather ball-making family who was a caddie and engaged in many big money matches, is described in a poem by J. F. Carnegie, written about 1830, as:
'Davie, oldest of the cads' and, in another line,
'Great Davie Robertson, the eldest cad'.

Carnegie was a regular golfer and would have been familiar with the name given to a caddie in his time but, here again, the question of poetic licence must be taken into consideration.

▷ *Corporal Sharp, a water colour by C. E. Cundell painted in 1839. This is the earliest portrait of a professional golfer. Sharp was, certainly, a professional caddie as well. His clothing suggests 'cast-offs' from the gentlemen for whom he carried. Note the clubs carried under the arm. The windmill in the background is one of the many that abounded on Blackheath Common at that time.*

C.E.Liddell

Corporal Sharp — 1839.

△ 'Old Alick', a portrait of Alick Brotherston, 1839, for many years a holecutter and caddie at Royal Blackheath Golf Club. His clothes suggest that he received gifts of 'cast-off' clothing to help him. One of the implements in his right hand is, probably, a putter. The other may be an instrument for cutting holes; this is not the usual instrument for the job but the holes at Blackheath were notoriously difficult to cut, owing to the underlying gravel. This is another painting by C. E. Cundell.

CADDIES

The first use of the word 'caddie' is in the account of Andrew Dickson of Leith, ball-maker and caddie (1655-1729), who ran forward to mark the balls for the Duke of York (later to be James II) when the Duke lived in Edinburgh and was playing in a match for large stakes.

Poetic licence or not, there seem to be four possible names by which those who carried clubs may have been known before the term caddie became universal. It is interesting that, although the term 'caddie' has now entered the language, there is no such verb as 'to caddy'; in England and, no doubt, overseas, golfers freely talk of 'caddying' although, strictly speaking, there is no such word. In general, they maintain the tradition in Scotland: caddies 'carry' clubs and when employed are said to be 'carrying'.

As the centre of the golfing world in the early 18th century was in the Edinburgh area, mainly at Leith and at Bruntsfield, what could be more natural than that the cadies or cawdys of Edinburgh should add carrying of golf clubs to their repertoire? It was likely also that they would continue to have some sort of Constable of the Cadies in charge of them, such as a caddie master. As we shall see, this official, originally appointed by the caddies themselves, subsequently came to be appointed by the Golf Club, who gave him their backing in the control of the caddies.

The reader must not think that the Edinburgh caddies were the first; caddies, by whatever name they were known, have probably existed since golf began — which will be well before 1450 — because there must have been friends of golfers or sons of golfers who, for little or no reward, helped out those who, by reason of age or infirmity, had difficulty in completing a round of golf while carrying their own clubs. When the Royal House of Stuart and the Royal Court 'took to the golf' they would have expected caddies to carry for them and would have been willing to pay a wage.

Thomas Kincaid and Sir James Foulis both paid money for caddies in the 17th century; they do not refer to them as caddies but as 'boys'. It is possible that the terms already mentioned for those who carried clubs stem from the era of the Edinburgh cadie and that, before that time, those who carried were simply referred to as 'boys'. In Foulis' accounts the boy was paid two shillings on one occasion, and four shillings on another, while Thomas Kincaid records a payment of three shillings.

2. THE EARLY DAYS

We now move forward to the era of the Golf Club, meaning organised groups of golfers, who had a clubhouse in which to change, who played matches and competitions and who maintained both the clubhouse and the links at their own, corporate, expense. The era began with the formation of the Company of Edinburgh Golfers who, in 1744, built a clubhouse at Leith where they played golf on the links.

The organisation of these clubs required the employment of club

servants. One group of servants looked after the clubhouse and the needs of the golfers off the links and were known, collectively, as the Indoor Staff. The other group, the Outdoor Staff, consisted of the keeper of the green, apprentices, professional players, professional caddies and the children who carried when not at school, and the labourers on the links.

▽ *A group of caddies at Westward Ho! toward the end of the 19th century. The clubs are probably their own and it is likely that this is the conclusion of one of the caddie competitions. The variety of clothing and head gear suggests donations from both family and golfers. Hobnail boots, also known as 'Tackety boots' are in evidence in the front row.*

THE KEEPER OF THE GREEN

At the time of the formation of Golf Clubs, the keeper of the green was of some importance. He was a man who had served his time as an apprentice club-maker, who had an ability both to play and to teach others to play and who had a knowledge of golf links and how to look after them.

The term 'Green' meant the whole golf links and not, as today, the putting greens. The keeper had a workshop in which he made clubs and balls, assisted there by a number of apprentices. He gave lessons, played in games with the members, was in overall charge of the professional caddies and of the various school children who carried clubs when they could get away from school in order to earn a few pence but who could not be dignified by the title 'professional'. The keeper was in charge of the labourers who worked on the links and was responsible to the club members for the proper care of the links. Because of his importance he was the only member of the outdoor staff who received a regular wage; he could, of course, make additional money by selling clubs and balls, and by playing with members and by giving lessons.

◁A group of caddies at Prestwick, c. 1880. They wear ill fitting and patched clothing and a variety of caps. Those who are not wearing cumbersome boots are barefoot. They are either watching a game or are waiting outside the caddie master's shed in the hope of getting a job.

PROFESSIONAL CADDIES

Many of the caddies were schoolboys but they could only carry when they were free of school and, in any event, few of them intended to make carrying a career. The professional caddies, on the other hand, were mostly grown men and had made carrying a career. There were black sheep among them, some were alcoholics, or were men who did not like regular work and found this an easy way out, but many made a career of this work and took a pride in their skill at finding balls, showing the line of a putt, giving their master the right club and, generally, helping him to play his best and win his matches.

They were of all ages, many were old men but some were young; from among the latter there would be one or two who had taught themselves to play well, or who had an aptitude for club-making or, perhaps, both. It was from these that the keeper of the green selected his apprentices and took them on in his shop to learn club-making, or ball-making; those who were skilful golfers might be allowed to play with members, if asked.

Most of the caddies had a pretty lean time in the winter, when little golf was played, and many took other jobs to tide them over until spring came and they were able to resume carrying. The professional caddies usually had a 'regular' for whom they invariably carried; in this way the caddie got to know his master's play and the golfer got to know his caddie, the two formed a team and established a rapport on the links and a long-standing friendship off it. This friendship between men from very different walks of life was classless and was particularly Scottish; it did not extend to England.

The closeness of a golfer and his caddie benefitted both, the former was helped to play better golf because the latter understood his strengths and his weaknesses and the caddie benefitted materially; apart from his fee, his master would make him gifts of cast-off clothing and consequently, over the years, the caddie came to have a resemblance to his master. Two examples serve to underline the importance to the caddie of these gifts.

A rather bad golfer went to the caddie master and asked for a caddie, the caddie that he got was a very experienced man who was usually in demand by the good golfers. When this golfer had played a number of rounds, it dawned upon him that he always got the same caddie. He said to the caddie 'I notice that you always make yourself available to carry for me, I am a very poor golfer and it seems to me that you would be better carrying for a good golfer, why do you continue to carry for me?' To this the caddy replied 'I have been looking

for a man like yourself for a long time. I am thinking that your clothes would be a perfect fit for me!'

On one occasion, a local caddie at St Andrews was carrying for a visitor from North Berwick. In the course of the round the golfer asked the caddie if he had ever carried for any famous men. 'Lots of them,' said the caddie, and went on to mention Mr A. J. Balfour; Mr Balfour was not only a very good amateur golfer but was, at that time, the Prime Minister. The caddie said that he had carried for Mr Balfour regularly, and had a very close acquaintance with him. The golfer, amused by the caddie's presumptuousness, asked him exactly what he meant by a 'close acquaintance'. 'Joost this', said the caddie, 'I am weering a pair o' Mr Balfour's troosers!'

In Scotland the professional caddie and the professional player were of the same status and were often the same person. In the first Open Championship in 1860 it was stipulated that 'competitors must be honest and respectable cadies'. It was further stipulated that each must have a letter from his club testifying to this. This last stipulation made sure that only the true professional caddies played, thus eliminating the casuals and all those who were too fond of the bottle.

◁*A player and his caddie in 1860. The player is General Sir Hope Grant, Adjutant General to the Army; although never a great player he was a keen supporter of golf. He had learned to play at St Andrews, where his father was a long-standing member. He was Captain of Prestwick in 1861 and was a frequent visitor to Westward Ho! (where he gave a Gold Medal which is still played for), St Andrews, Blackheath and Prestwick. In this posed photograph he appears to be holding a putting cleek. All the other clubs that the caddie carries seem to be wooden ones. Both player and caddie have buttoned up coats; the caddie's coat is shabby but well cut and may well be a present from his master's wardrobe.*

Genral Grant had two brothers. One of them was Sir Francis Grant PRA. At a party, a lady, talking to the third brother, said: 'Sir, you have one brother who is a famous soldier and one brother who is a famous artist, pray, what are you?' To which he replied: 'Madam, I am something which neither of my brothers can ever be — I am the oldest brother!'

3.FORECADDIES

D uring the 19th century there were two types of caddie on the course, the forecaddie and the carrying caddie. The latter was the senior and the more experienced. The job of the forecaddie was to see where the ball went; in those days there were many more blind holes than exist today and the feather ball was expensive. Additionally, if the feather ball fell into the water, it had to be removed quickly – immersion even for a short time would convert the ball into a soggy mass of feathers.

Because of the blind holes, forecaddies were further divided into 'moving' forecaddies and 'fixed'

△ *The British Amateur Championship, 1928. The wall at Prestwick separating the first fairway from the railway line. The forecaddie sits astride the wall, with a piece of sacking over his head and shoulders to keep off the rain. The white flag signals that the ball is on the fairway; the red (dark) flag that it is 'out of bounds' on the railway.*

△ *The 'Maiden' (6th hole) at Royal St Georges, Sandwich, 1892. The green is over the hill. The forecaddie stands atop the hill and will signal when the players in front have cleared the green. There is no sand tee box; sand for tees would have been taken from the previous hole.*

forecaddies. The latter would remain on the top of the hill over which the blind shot was to be played and would not only mark where the ball went but would signal to the waiting players when it was safe to play without danger of hitting the people in front.

MOVING FORECADDIES

The moving forecaddie walked with the players and would walk up the fairway to the point which, he considered, his master would reach if he hit his usual shot and would then stand and wait for the ball. If the shot

19

△ *Another view of the 'Maiden' (6th hole) at Royal St Georges Golf Club, Sandwich. The players, having driven over the hill, are now putting on the green. The fixed forecaddie on the hill behind has his flag flying to indicate to the players on the tee that it is not safe to drive yet. A forecaddie from the match behind has also climbed on to the hill.*

was much off course the player or his carrying caddie would signal the direction. Occasionally, the forecaddie would underestimate the distance that his master hit the ball, in which case, if he failed to see it coming, he could be hit. Francis Powell Hopkins, the earliest journalist to write about golf, describes such an incident in the *Field* in 1873. One pair in a match were, he notes, 'driving exceptionally well, and the forecaddies rubbing their stomachs'.

When an accident of this sort was likely to occur the player would warn the forecaddie by shouting 'Forecaddie!' In time, the warning

▷ *A Blackheath scene of 1875. The player is attempting to drive over one of the ravines, the fixed forecaddie on the far side having indicated that it is safe to play. Note the roughness of the ground compared with the immaculate fairways of modern courses. One of the many lamp-posts on the Common is in the background, behind the forecaddie.*

was shortened to 'Fore!', 'Forecaddie' being a bit of a mouthful when one is in a hurry. This is the origin of the warning shout, peculiar to golfers, which indicates to anyone nearby that they are in danger of being hit.

On courses on public ground, forecaddies were useful to warn the public of possible danger when they were crossing the links. As an additional warning the golfers wore red coats; these red coats were less in evidence in Scotland than in England. In England there were many who, crossing a golf course, had no idea of golf, of the distance that a golf ball could be hit, nor of the pain that a full drive could inflict, whereas, in Scotland, where all the links were

near villages and the inhabitants were probably golfers themselves, no warning red coat was necessary.

Describing a match in which he took part at Royal Blackheath Golf Club in about 1910, Bernard Darwin writes that he and his opponent went off 'for all the world, like two steam rollers' (an allusion to the days when it was obligatory for steam rollers to be preceded by a man carrying a red flag).

An experienced forecaddie was an expert. Bob Ferguson of Musselburgh was a caddie who won the Open Championship in 1880, 1881 and 1882; he then became very ill with typhoid and never fully recovered. As a result, he was never

able to compete again and supported himself by carrying at Musselburgh, his home course and the scene of one of his Open triumphs. He gives a vivid description of being a forecaddie:

> My first job was as a forecaddie and, I daresay it was two years before I was promoted to carrying caddie. We used to get two shillings a day when acting as a forecaddie, with a lunch at Mrs Foreman's, consisting of fourpence worth of bread and cheese [Mrs Foreman's was a public house adjacent to the links at Musselburgh; it is still there]. Those were happy days, running as forecaddies to mark down the ball, as well as showing the line to the hole, for, in those days there were no flags in the holes at Musselburgh. We had to learn a few simple signals to make the golfers acquainted with the kind of lies their ball had secured. They were very impatient, these old golfers; and as there was nearly always a wager on the match, you could not let them know too soon what their chances were of winning or losing the hole. If the ball landed in decent country the forecaddie had to face about towards the players and stroke his breast downward with his right hand. If the ball fell in the whins [gorse] or bunker, the mishap was telegraphed by a downward stroke of the right fist held outward from

the body; two downward strokes indicated that the lie was very bad indeed. A downward stroke and a gentle motion of the hand from right to left indicated that the ball was lying in a hazard but lying, hopefully, on a smooth surface. It was the duty of the forecaddie, when a ball fell among whins, to mark the place with a piece of paper — which was liftable, of course, by the player — and then hurry off to take up a fresh stand.

FIXED FORECADDIES

The fixed forecaddie, of course, did not walk round with the players but remained in one spot, often armed with a red flag, waved the players when it was safe to play and then watched the ball.

A fixed forecaddie's functions could be varied according to local needs. Such a man was employed at Prestwick Golf Club. He rejoiced in the name of Tweedly and was

▷ *Golf at Prestwick. The dress is typical of mid 19th-century golfers. 'Norfolk jackets' are worn buttoned up, as was customary. The caddie has the same costume as the players and has the clubs tucked under his arm. The large sand box is made of wood.*

◁*Medal Day at Blackheath, 1875. Everyone is tense as the player tries to carry the gravel pit. On the far side is a fixed forecaddie with a flag. To his right, in the background, is the Dover to London coach.*

stationed on a bridge over the Pow Burn; at this point the players had to play blind over a sand dune and the Burn which was on the other side of the dune and thus out of sight. Tweedly's position on the bridge meant that he could not see the balls coming over until they were almost on top of him and, to make matters worse, he was supposed to mark the splash where the ball went in, so that he had to concentrate on the water rather than the sky. It was a post of some danger and he was often hit, so he took to wearing an old straw beehive as a hat, which gave him some protection.

At Westward Ho! there is a 'burn' in front of the 18th green; it was the job of Kelly, nicknamed 'Dandino', to

▷ *'Dandino' Kelly's hut at the 18th at Westward Ho! The 'burn' and its bridge can be seen on the left; on the right is the 18th green and flagstick. The village in the background is Appledore.*

The second shot is a long one played from the left; Kelly's job was to pick the balls of those who failed to carry the burn out of the water and he combined this with acting as greenkeeper to the 18th green. The hut gave him protection from those who sliced their second shots.

Kelly's brother was the Steward at Royal North Devon Golf Club. Although the hut is no longer there the scene is, otherwise, exactly the same.

watch for the balls as players attempted to carry the burn. He was rather better off than Tweedly as the club gave him a sort of wooden sentry box in which he could take shelter. As well as watching for balls in the burn Dandino Kelly also maintained the 18th green and kept it in good order.

Darwin, writing of the 1880s and 1890s, remembers forecaddies but could not recall any signals. However, he remembered with nostalgic pleasure the cry of 'on the green!' from a forecaddie perched on a sandhill known as Cader at Aberdovey as the ball sailed over the top, and the opposite when a small French boy shouted 'A Bayonne!' as a ball was engulfed by the river Gare at Pau in south-west France.

FORECADDIES – THE END?

Forecaddies were banned by the R & A in 1956, thus at one stroke of the pen creating fear in the breast of all those who had to play a blind shot over a hill on medal days in a strong cross wind. No reason was given for this decision but it clearly must have been because of the possibility of unofficial help from a forecaddie with a bet on the outcome of the match who, when out of sight of the players, ensured that his master had a good lie. At one time there was a saying in golf that 'a man with three forecaddies never loses a ball'.

A player, playing a practice round, found that his good tee shot was in a terrible lie and said to his caddie 'If I got a lie like this in tomorrow's competition I would be most disappointed!' to which the caddie replied darkly 'If this was tomorrow you wouldn't have a bad lie.'

Although the forecaddie is officially banned he is still with us; in many major golf competitions a long-suffering club member is often stationed on some draughty promontory where there is a blind shot, his job being to wave players on when it is safe to play and keep an eye on the ball.

Forecaddies abound in major professional competitions, a famous professional will have perhaps a thousand of them, all scampering down the fairway and manning the rough in order to watch him play. If a man with three forecaddies never lost a ball, a man with a thousand forecaddies can have no worries on that score.

As a last comment on forecaddies, a friend of mine (who was there) tells of two well-known professionals who were due to give an exhibition match at Royal Colombo Golf Club in about 1948. In the practice round, they came to a short hole where it was necessary to play over a large pond. In the pond stood a forecaddie, almost up to his shoulders in water, waiting to rescue the balls of those unfortunates who failed to carry it. The professionals had difficulty in judging the distance; one struck his ball over the back of the green and the other put his in the pond. One said to the other 'I can't seem to get the distance right.' One of the spectators suggested that, perhaps, Ali, the forecaddie, could help and they called him from his station in the pond. He emerged, dripping wet and clad only in a

▷ *An advertisement for H. Pattison and Co., c. 1910. The company was one of the pioneers in manufacturing accessories for golf courses. Spring flagsticks were very useful on courses which* *had sheep on them because the flagsticks 'gave' when the sheep rubbed against them and thus did not snap. The flagsticks were also able to bend in the strong winds on the seaside courses.*

loincloth. After he had dried his hands, he said something in his native tongue which was immediately translated by the spectators as a request for a No 3. iron; he borrowed a club and ball from one of the pros, teed up and struck the ball into the middle of the green. There was some clapping and cheering; encouraged, he put down two more balls and put both of them into the middle of the green. At this stage one of the professionals seized the club from him and said, 'OK, OK, get back in the swamp, mate. I give the exhibitions round here!'

Steel Spring Flag Staffs.

The principal objection to sheep being grazed on Golf Courses is their habit of using the rigid Flagstaffs as rubbing posts, thus involving great damage to the Greens, and much extra labour for the Greenkeeper. The " PATTISSON" Spring Staffs quickly cure this habit, as they yield immediately to pressure and rebound, which is what the animal does not want. The **Springs are very strong** being made of the **best quality spring Steel**, and are very durable. The small extra cost is quickly repaid by the **improved condition of the Greens**, and the **reduced amount of work** required on them.

The Staffs, up to 8 feet high, are made of Steel, as per Fig. 11 ; above 8 feet, of Steel Tube or Bamboo above the Spring, as Figs. 12 and 14. They are **very strong, and yet light.**

The Fig. 11 **SPRING STAFFS** can be **strongly recommended even where there are no sheep, as light and most effective Pins**, particularly on windy courses, as they ' give ' to the wind and there is little strain on the tins.

WICKER BALLOONS, fitted to Spring Staffs, as Fig. 15 are the same prices as given below for Steel Balloons.

FIG. 11.

FIG. 13

PRICES—**Steel**, as per Woodcut, Fig. 11

						3 feet high,	3s. 0d. each
,,	,,	,,	,,			4 ,, ,,	4s. 0d. ,,
,,	,,	,,	,,			5 ,, ,,	4s. 6d. ,,
,,	,,	,,	,,			6 ,, ,,	5s. 0d. ,,
,,	,,	,,	,,			7 ,, ,,	5s. 6d. ,,
,,	,,	,,	,,			8 ,, ,,	6s. 0d. ,,

Bamboo Staff, fitted above heavy Spring, Fig. 12

					9 ,, ,,	6s. 6d. ,,
,,	,,	,,	,,		10 ,, ,,	7s. 0d. ,,
,,	,,	,,	,,		12 ,, ,,	7s. 6d. ,,

Steel Tube Staffs, above heavy Spring, Fig. 14, without Balloon

					9 ,, ,,	7s. 6d. ,,
,,	,,	,,	,,	,,	10 ,, ,,	8s. 0d. ,,
,,	,,	,,	,,	,,	12 ,, ,,	8s. 6d. ,,

Small Balloon Flags are fitted to light Springs, Price, 4 ft., 6s. 6d. ; 5 ft., 7s. 0d. ; 6ft., 8s. 0d. ; complete. See Fig. 13.

Large Balloons and 3 and 4-wing **Steel Flags** are fitted to heavy Springs, up to 6 ft. in height, as per Fig. 14.

PRICES—**Balloons** (Fig. 14 and 15) ... 4 ft., 8s. 0d.; 5 ft., 8s. 6d.; 6 ft., 9s. 0d.
  Three Wing Flags (Fig. 2, page 13) ,, 6s. 6d.; ,, 7s. 0d.; ,, 7s. 6d.
  Four ,, ,, (,, 7 ,, 13) ,, 6s. 6d.; ,, 7s.0d.; ,, 7s. 6d.

FIG 12. Fig. 15.

FIG. 14.

W. A. FAWAIS, Esq. (Mullion Golf Club) writes :—" The Spring Flag Staffs are a great success."
W. E. PICKERING, Esq. (Knavesmire Golf Club) writes :—" The Spring Staffs are very satisfactory."
GURNEY COOMBS, Esq. (Arundel Golf Club) writes :—" I am pleased to say the Spring Staffs have been most satisfactory."
Major C. J. LLOYD CARSON (Leamington & County Golf Club) writes :—" The Spring Staffs previously supplied are excellent. Nothing could be better where sheep have to be dealt with."

RULES

REGARDING

PAY AND DISCIPLINE OF CADDIES,

ADOPTED BY

THE ROYAL AND ANCIENT GOLF CLUB OF ST. ANDREWS,

At a Special General Meeting of the Club, held on 3rd February, 1875.

I.—All Caddies shall be Enrolled,—none being admitted under 13 years of age.

II.—Members of the Club shall employ only Enrolled Caddies.

III.—A List of Enrolled Caddies shall be placed in the Club Hall, and also in the Clubmakers' Shops.

IV.—Caddies shall be divided into Two Classes, according to skill or age, and their services shall be rated as follows:—

First Class Caddies,—Eighteenpence for First Round, and One Shilling for each following Round, or part of Round.

Second Class Caddies,—One Shilling for First Round, and Sixpence for each following Round, or part of Round.

V.—No Caddy, unless previously engaged, can refuse to carry for a Member, under penalty of suspension for a stated time.

VI.—Names of suspended or disqualified Caddies shall be posted.

VII.—Complaints regarding Caddies shall be made through the Keeper of the Green to the Green Committee, who shall award an adequate penalty.

VIII.—The penalty shall be awarded by not less than two of the Green Committee.

IX.—The Keeper of the Green shall have charge of the Caddies, and Members shall apply to him when in want of a Caddy.

X.—Members are particularly urged to report all cases of misconduct on the part of the Caddies, whether during their time of service or otherwise,—such as incivility, bad language, abusing the Green, or any other form of misdemeanour—which may merit censure or penalty.

XI.—Tom Morris shall be Keeper of the Green, and Superintendent of the Caddies.

4. CARRYING CADDIES

It goes without saying that there were good carrying caddies and bad ones. The bad ones were the very elderly and slow, those who drank too much, and the young boys who could not be bothered to see where the ball went, fidgeted and moved about on the tee when people were playing and generally gave evidence of larking about and not paying attention. These caddies were graded as 'Second Class'.

The First Class caddie was a valued helper who carried out a number of duties. Firstly, he carried the clubs, usually under his arm, occasionally on his shoulder — there were no golf bags until about 1889. On the tee, he made a tee of sand and teed the ball up, having, either by past experience or by judicious questioning on the first tee, found out what height of tee his master preferred. He gave his master the necessary club, having ensured that the grip was dry and the club face clean. If asked, he would advise as to the best line and which was the right club, basing his advice on how the ball was lying and on his knowledge of the player's weaknesses and strengths. He would take the flag on the putting green and, if asked, advise on the line of the putt.

At the end of the round he would take the clubs to the caddies' shed where he would dry the shafts and clean the heads; there was no such thing as stainless steel and the iron heads had to be cleaned with a fine emery paper and then wiped over with a slightly oily rag. After this he would take the clubs back to the clubhouse.

For these onerous duties he would be paid between sixpence and one shilling a round, often with a deduction if his master lost a ball. The Second Class caddie would be paid less.

Sir Walter Simpson, a keen but rather mediocre player in the mid 19th century, was a man of some humour. He wrote *The Art of Golf* (1892) and had some amusing things to say about caddies. He mentions that some people call them 'caudies' and that some try to do without them but expresses the opinion that even a bad one is better than none. He points out that caddies are a miscellaneous bunch being, he says, boys, ragamuffins just out of prison, workmen out of a job and professional carriers. He recommends the last. He goes on to say:

◁*An attempt to control the caddies. It did not work during Tom Morris' time because he was sympathetic to them and a friend of many.*

▷ *This sturdy boy with no shoes and ragged clothes is typical of the young boy caddies of the mid 19th century. He carries the clubs, mostly wooden, on his shoulder, which, perhaps, shows his inexperience. One suspects that he was a 'Second Class' caddie.*

◁ *Caddies' list at St Andrews, c. 1870. Among the names on the list are those of three Open Champions: Willie Fernie (1883), Thomas Kidd Junior (1873), Robert Martin (1876 and 1885).*

Carrying clubs is one of the most agreeable trades open to the lower orders. In it an amount of drunkenness is tolerated which, in any other, would land him in the workhouse. [The workhouse was an institution which housed vagrants, the poor and the homeless on the condition that they carried out the work necessary to keep the institution going; it was not uncommon for magistrates to send people to the workhouse for minor offences such as drunkenness, rather than commit them to prison.] A very low standard of efficiency and very little work will secure a man a decent livelihood. If he is civil, willing to work for three or four hours a day and not apt to drink to excess before his work is done, he will earn a fair wage.

This rather lordly and contemptuous attitude to caddies is that of an employer who considers such riff-raff lucky to be allowed to caddie for him.

Andrew Kirkaldy, a great professional golfer and Keeper of the Green at St Andrews in the early part of the 20th century, was a caddie when he was a lad. He gives a different viewpoint on caddies. In his book of reminiscences, *Fifty Years of Golf* (1921), he says that a caddie who carried regularly for his master knew him well and that a wise golfer would do well to heed his advice and treat him fairly.

At St Andrews, in particular, many of the caddies were fishermen; they often played golf themselves and were very knowledgeable but regarded carrying as something to do when they could not fish. They called carrying 'grass hoppin' ', or 'workin' on the land'.

Kirkaldy points out that they would pour scorn on anyone who was a poor golfer and exercise their wit at his expense but would give considerable help and loyalty to those who appreciated it and that, as a result, a golfer would insist on having the same caddie for round after round.

◁ *The caddies' shelter at St Andrews. The caddies wear good strong boots and a variety of tweed coats.*

Overleaf *A stymie occurs when one ball blocks the line of another to the hole. Under today's Rules of Golf the obstructing ball may be lifted — a rule more recent than this picture!*

"Stymied!"

▽ *Golf at Westward Ho!, 1875. The caddie wears a 'Tam o' Shanter'. As golf began in Scotland, the Scottish form of head gear was common in England.*

THE TASK IN HAND

The making of a sand tee

In the early 19th century golf was played on 'links' courses; these were sandy areas near the sea. There was a thin covering of turf under which was sand. When a hole was cut, the rim was turf but the rest was sand and there was, of course, no 'tin' in the hole. The hole was about 5-7 paces from the next 'tee', the latter being simply a suitable flat piece of turf. The sand used for teeing up the ball was taken from the bottom of the hole; as a result, a hole which was a neat 4½ inches in diameter when cut was a ragged edged hole 6 inches in diameter within a few days.

It might be thought that sand was taken from the hole because it was near the next tee and because the caddie was lazy, but this was not so;

clubs insisted that sand be taken from holes. In 1870 there was an edict from the Secretary of the Elie and Earlsferry Golf Club:

> The destruction caused to the green [meaning the course] by the prevalent practice of taking sand for tees from the course, instead of from the hole, is becoming so serious that the Committee feel impelled, in the interests of the game, to request that all golfers will abstain from this pernicious practice and will positively prohibit their caddies from infringing this Regulation.

Those caddies who did not take sand from the hole usually carried round a small canvas sack containing sand. This may have been simply to have sand readily available but it is much more likely to have been because the sand in the canvas sacks would have been well wetted before starting out – making a sand tee is much easier with wet sand than with the dry, powdery variety.

Toward the end of the 19th century iron tee boxes appeared on what were, by then, well defined teeing grounds some distance from the green; these tee boxes were filled with sand. The more de luxe tee boxes had a small reservoir of water at the top which dripped water into the sand and thus kept it moist. Few golfers today realise that the square iron tee boxes which still exist on some of our older

▽ *Catalogue of H.* | *tee boxes are shown.* | *keep the sand moist,* | *Brushes can be fitted,*
Pattisson and Co. | *Several have a water* | *thus enabling a sand tee* | *as an extra, to clean the*
c. 1910. A variety of | *reservoir attached to* | *to be made more easily.* | *ball.*

Sand (and Water) Boxes.

LIGHT, STRONG AND DURABLE.

Our **1st Quality** Boxes are strongly made of Black **Steel Plate**, and **Galvanized after Rivetting.** These Boxes are **much stronger, more durable,** and therefore **more economical,** than any made up with Galvanized Sheet Iron, or Zinc, which can easily be sold at a lower price. Figs. 1 and 2 are also supplied as Water Boxes, with or without .ids. In hot weather the water is useful for moistening the Sand and in muddy weather for washing Balls.

FIG. 1.

For **Water Boxes** to hang on to Sand Boxes see Figs. 1A and 2A. (Either of these Boxes will last many years.)

The **Fig. 1 and Fig. 2** Boxes are also supplied in **B Quality** at lower prices. These are made of lighter Steel Plate (ungalvanized). They are well painted inside and out, and although not equal to our 1st Quality **are good boxes of exactly the same sizes.**

FIG. 1A.

Fig. 4a is of Special Quality with a Water Tank fixed to it, as shewn below. The latter is fitted with a Brass Screw Plug so that **the dirty water can be run off** in a few seconds. It can be fitted with a ball brush if required. This Sand Box is larger and of heavier plate than our Fig. 2 pattern, and will last a lifetime.

Fig. 4 is the same Box, minus the Water Tank. *See* woodcut.

The finest and most expensive quality of English Paint used, for all Boxes, Flags, etc. Any required colour used.

FIG. 2.

FIG. 2A.

PRICES.

Fig. 1, **1st Quality** (13 in. square at base, 6 in. at top, 8½ each. in. high), extra well painted, White or Red Enamel **5/-**
„ 2, **1st Quality Square** (10 in. square, 12 in. high) ditto **5/-**
„ 3, **Round** (10 in. diam., 12 in. high) ditto **3/3**
„ 4, **Square, Extra Strong** (12 in. square, 12 in. high)... **10/6**
„ 4A, „ „ „ **with water tank** **12/6**
Steel Water Boxes, to hang on to Figs. 1 or 2 Sand Boxes, as shewn in Figs. 1a and 2a **3/6**
Ball Brushes for Water Boxes ... ... **-/6**
Fig. 1, **B Quality Pyramid Steel Boxes** **4/-**
„ 2, B „ Square „ „ **4/-**
Wood Tee Boxes—Made of best Elm (very substantial), 1½ in. thick, painted with 4 coats of best Enamel **5/-**
Feet for Steel Sand Boxes—Wrought Iron. **9d.** per pair.
Handles for Steel and Wood Sand Boxes—Malleable Wrought Iron. **8d.** per pair. See Fig. 4.
Lids fitted to Figs. 1 and 2, **1/-** each extra.
BOLD IRON FIGURES (2¼ ins. high) as Numbers to fix to Boxes or Steel Flags, 3/- per dozen.

FIG. 3.

WOOD.

FIG. 4.

SAND BOX FEET.

FIG. 4A

LETTERS AND FIGURES ON NEW BOXES.

Initials of Club in bold letters, **2d.** per letter, or **8/6** the set of 18 Boxes.
Numbers 1 to 18, in bold figures **2d.** per figure, or **4/-** the set of 18 Boxes.

Lengths of Holes, 6d. per Box.
Bogey 4, Etc., **6d.** per Box.
"Turf Must be Replaced," Etc., **6d.** per Box.

J. F. MARKES, Esq. (Sandy Lodge G.C.)—"All the goods are quite satisfactory. The Sand Boxes with water tanks and brushes have been much admired by Members and Visitors, and I hope this will result in you getting orders for them from other Clubs."
Mr. W. BUTTON (Sutton-on-Sea G.C.) writes—"My Committee are more than satisfied with all the goods supplied by your firm."
Mr. J. GOWANS, Senr. (Worlingham G.C.) writes—" The Boxes are highly satisfactory."
Mr. G. M. HARVEY (Horsham G.C.) writes—"Everything (Tins, Cutters, Boxes, &c.) is very satisfactory."
P. GRAY, Esq. (North Cornwall G.C.) writes—"We are very pleased with the Steel Sand Boxes."
Rev. JOHN LINDSAY (Bathgate G.C.) writes—"The Sand Boxes have, as before, given every satisfaction."

◁ *Political golfing cartoon, c. 1890. A. J. Balfour MP, later Prime Minister, was a very good golfer.*

△ *Making a sand tee, 1890. The caddie seems to be too well dressed to be a professional.*

courses were not designed to hold, as they do today, golf ball wrappers and other plastic debris, but sand for making tees.

The caddie would make a tee of sand at the spot where his master tapped the tee with his club; the caddie would know, if he had carried for the golfer before, what height of tee he preferred.

Sir Walter Simpson, writing in his rather lordly style about the qualities of a good caddie, says that he should not make a tee more than 2 inches in diameter and, 'if each time a club is required, he is not more than three minutes walk from his master, if he knows the names of the clubs [Note: Not the numbers!] then he is a good caddie.'

John Henry Taylor of Westward Ho!, later in life to be five times Open Champion, started carrying at Westward Ho! as a small boy. He says

◁ *A woodcut from a picture by F. P. Hopkins, c. 1870. Some ingenuity on the links at Westward Ho! in North Devon. The tent in the background was used as a clubhouse; Bideford Bay and the great pebble ridge can be seen behind it. The player seems to be expecting the caddie to show devotion to duty of an unusually high order. The amused spectator is the artist. In 1870 this idea would have been regarded as an ingenious solution — even if it did not work; there were then only 13 Rules of Golf. The present day 72-page booklet would condemn the idea as illegal.*

that his first master was a 'real Tartar' but he (Taylor) was always grateful to him because he took the trouble to go down on his knees and show the little boy exactly how he liked his tee made.

A good caddie learnt all sorts of tricks to help his master; at short holes, a clever caddie would, after completing the tee, place the ball on top and, in doing so, cause a few grains of sand to adhere to a well licked thumb, which he then smeared on to the back of the ball, thus helping his master to get a little more backspin.

This practice of having the caddie make a sand tee gradually died out, a process accelerated by the invention of the wooden 'peg' tee in the early 1930s. Nevertheless, the custom persisted overseas for many years, although it never really started in the United States of America, where, from the beginning, American golfers preferred to tee the ball up themselves.

In the 1950s Bobby Locke came over from South Africa where he had been accustomed to the caddie teeing the ball up for him; the custom was still sufficiently common in this country for his caddie to know what was required, but when he went to play in the USA his caddie, of course, did not. It is said that he tapped the tee with his driver but his caddie took no notice, he tapped the tee again — again nothing happened. He then told the caddie to tee the ball up, the surprised caddie did so but while crouched over the ball, he looked up and said to Locke 'Ah sure hope yo' back gwine to get better soon, or we ain't goin' to make no money!'

The carrying of clubs

Golf clubs were taken from place to place in wooden boxes. Until about 1888 there were no golf bags, when the clubs were removed from the golf box they were held together by a leather strap. When taken on the links the leather strap was removed and the clubs were carried under the arm.

It is not known when, or where, golf bags were invented. John Henry Taylor of Westward Ho! claimed that they were invented at Westward Ho! when he was a boy caddie in about 1880. The first Steward at Royal North Devon Golf Club was Bryant Andrews; he took the job because he could no longer go to sea as a sailor and sailmaker. He made the canvas tent, which was the first clubhouse and, according to Taylor, he made some narrow canvas bags which could be carried from the shoulder and which would prevent the clubs' grips getting wet when it rained. Taylor records how, at first, the older caddies did not like the idea and carried the bag under one arm and the clubs under the other. Pictures of the older caddies in about 1890 show that they used the new golf bags but carried the bag under the arm, not by the strap from the shoulder.

△ Dr Siddall, c. 1890. Watched with interest by his caddie, who carries the clubs tucked under his arm, Siddall is putting in a style that Sam Snead used about 100 years later. There is nothing new in golf!

◁ 'Pawky' Corstorphine in front of the Caddie Master's office, c. 1920. The Caddie Master is looking out of the window. Note the bag, carried under the arm, in the old tradition.

The cleaning of clubs

All golf clubs had hickory shafts and if these got very wet the shaft could lose its spring permanently. This fact was the main reason for not playing on a very wet day and was a reason for drying and oiling a shaft after exposure to rain. Unlike the steel shaft of today, the matching of a new shaft to an old clubhead so as to give the same 'feel' was impossible, so time was given to caring for them.

The shaft of a wooden club, if wet, would be carefully dried and some linseed oil applied; the varnish would be examined to see if re-varnishing was necessary. The wooden head was not treated with linseed as it might open up the grain. The shaft of an iron club would be similarly treated and the head cleaned, as already described; nevertheless, there was a definite ritual to the cleaning. The hose was cleaned by putting the end of the shaft on the floor, wrapping the hose in emery paper and then rotating the head, keeping the disengaged hand on the toe of the club. The face of the club was cleaned by using the emery from heel to toe and back as often as was necessary; at the end, the centre of the face was rubbed with emery from upper to lower edge. As a result, when the player looked down on the face the centre would stand out and would show the sweetspot quite clearly.

In the first half of the 19th century the faces of iron clubs were all

smooth; later in the century, iron club faces were scored with grooves or dots to improve the grip of the club on the ball and thus allow the player to get more backspin. The fact that the iron club heads had to be cleaned with fine emery after each round resulted, after many years, in the grooves or dots disappearing; it also made the clubs lighter and affected the balance.

CADDIES' DRESS

The tradition that regular caddies got gifts of cast-off clothing from their masters has already been mentioned. Schoolboy caddies came from poor families and wore any old clothes that would keep them warm; often the clothes were too big, being cast-off clothes from their father or an elder

△ *The three Allan brothers playing at Westward Ho!, c. 1870. They came from Prestwick. Johnny Allan (on the left) was the professional and club-maker at Westward Ho! His two brothers were his assistants. The caddies have the clubs under their arms. The group is on the putting green, which is simply a flat piece of fairway. The caddie on the left holds a flagstick; before these were used the hole was marked by a seagull's feather stuck in the ground.*

△ *Cartoon by Sandercock, 1890. One caddie is barefoot;* *the other has the clubs encircled by a leather strap.*

brother. Frequently, they had no shoes or stockings. Mrs Williams of Westward Ho!, who was proud of the fact that she was a First Class caddie in about 1910, told me that she used to caddie barefoot but, with the arrival of motor cars, she had found that a piece of motor tyre, held on by string, served as a good shoe.

The regular caddie, wearing his master's cast-off clothing, looked rather better dressed but the clothes were invariably dirty and the mixture of clothes often lent him a bizarre appearance; this type of caddie was confined to Scotland. Few caddies in England made carrying a life-time's career.

The dirtiness of the caddies was sometimes so marked that those who employed them objected. At Prestwick Golf Club in 1890 members complained of the unwashed state of the caddies and Charles Hunter, who combined the duties of Keeper of the Green and Caddie Master, was called upon to inspect every caddie who presented himself for employment and not to allow the very unclean to carry.

PAY, TIPS AND PERKS

The remuneration of caddies varied from club to club and depended, to a certain extent, on the ready availability of caddies locally and whether demand exceeded supply, or vice versa.

The caddie fee also varied according to the caddie's grade. It goes without saying that the regular professional caddie was First Class and the schoolboys, casuals and those who only carried occasionally were in the Second Class.

At Prestwick in 1865 caddies were to be paid fourpence per round; by 1875 Second Class caddies were paid fourpence per round and First Class caddies were paid sixpence.

At St Andrews in 1873 caddies over twenty years of age were paid one shilling and sixpence for the first round and sixpence for the second; those under twenty were paid one shilling for the first round and sixpence for the second. Clearly St Andrews were willing to pay more for their caddies than Prestwick. Even so, both compare very unfavourably with the pay of caddies in the 17th century, when Foulis and Kincaid were prepared to pay two shillings and three shillings per round respectively.

— 'CARRY YOUR BAG, SIR?' —

▽ *Wimbledon Common,*   The caddies wear
near London, c. 1890.   bowler hats and shoes.

Probably this was because golf was
then a Royal Stuart game and
members of the Royal Court were
able to pay over the odds for a caddie.

The caddie, fortunately for him, did
not have to rely solely on his wage;
there was usually a tip, the size of
which depended on the competence of
the caddie, the success of the player
and the latter's generosity — or lack of
it. The size of the tip also depended on
whether the golfer was employing a

boy of school age, or an adult, professional caddie. Two anecdotes serve to underline the importance of a tip to a caddie.

At Prestwick, a player had had the services of a First Class caddie. At the end of the round he gave the caddie three pennies; the caddie laid them in the palm of his hand and said to the player, 'Sir, are ye aware I can tell yer fortune frae these three coins?' The player asked him to do so. 'The first one tells me y're no a Scotchman, am I richt?' The stranger nodded. 'An' the second that y're no merrit, am I richt?' Again the stranger nodded and asked about the third coin, 'Weel, the third yin, weel it joost tells me that y're faither wasna' merrit either.'

On a happier note, at Hoylake a player holed the old Rushes hole in one; he rewarded his caddie, a small boy, on the spot. The boy was so overcome that he dropped the clubs and rushed home to tell his mother, leaving his master to carry his own clubs.

Apart from his standard pay and a tip the regular, professional caddie in Scotland benefitted in other ways. Besides cast-off clothes, many regular caddies received food and, sometimes drink, from their employers. The master, too, would visit his caddie if he were sick, and was called upon from time to time to give advice and help to the caddie's family.

Sometimes, in order to help the caddie to earn a regular income, not least to tide him over the winter when there was little golf, his master would give him another job in his household. As a boy caddie, John Henry Taylor worked for Horace Hutchinson's father as a bootblack and general handyman. Mr Condie of Perth had Robert Andrews (nicknamed 'the Rook') as a caddie. The Rook was a very good professional golfer who played in the first eight Open Championships being third on two occasions and runner-up in 1868 — the eighth Open; he also won many money matches. Mr Condie, himself a very good amateur golfer, employed Andrews as a valet. Andrews carried for Condie and frequently played with him, as his partner, in foursome matches.

George Morris, Tom Morris senior's brother, was a caddie and professional; he got a job with Mr Robert Chambers of Edinburgh. Chambers employed Morris as his own personal professional and as a general handyman. Like Andrews, Morris played with his master in foursome matches as well as carrying for him.

These are merely two examples of many in Scotland but they serve to show the close master and man relationship which bridged the class gap in that country.

RULES AND REGULATIONS

Towards the end of the 19th century Golf Clubs began to show an interest in the welfare of their caddies. Clubs such as Prestwick and the R & A introduced regulations for the employment and payment of caddies; lists of caddies were posted in the clubhouse; a shelter was provided for them and an attempt was made to deal with truancy.

Truancy was a considerable problem, as small boys preferred to earn a few pennies as caddies rather than attend school. The superintendents of the local schools met with the secretaries and committees of Golf Clubs and, in many localities, regulations forbade children of school age carrying, except at weekends, public holidays and during school holidays. This by no means stopped all truancy but did bring the level below 60 per cent.

Golf Clubs made efforts to permit all the caddies to have some food and drink while working, but at Prestwick an edict went out from the Secretary, Mr Hart, that the practice of giving caddies biscuits in the middle of the day 'will be discontinued'. Any member engaging a caddie was to give his caddie a penny in lieu. A system of fines, not to exceed sixpence, was

▽ Boy caddies waiting for a carrying job outside the professional's shop at Lytham St Annes Golf Club. George Lowe was the professional.

△ *Littlestone Golf Club meal tokens.*

These were handed to caddies in lieu of tips.

introduced for misconduct, misbehaviour or inattentiveness. The fines were kept by the caddie master and, twice a year, the money collected was given as prizes to those junior caddies deemed to have the best attendance record at school and general good behaviour on the links.

At St Andrews a similar sort of scheme was introduced; a list of caddies was posted in the Clubhouse and there were regulations as to their duties and pay. It was ordained that each caddie had to have a ticket, wear a cap with the Club badge on it when on the links and, in the case of those under thirteen, continue his education and attend Sunday school. Additionally, he must not use bad language. At the beginning of the year, each caddie would deposit two shillings and

sixpence with the Club; at the end of the year, after deductions for the repair and upkeep of the Caddies' Shelter, the remaining money would be doubled by the Club and divided equally among all the caddies who had a blameless record. A fund was also started to provide clothing for the caddies.

Tom Morris senior was made Superintendent of Caddies, but in despite of all the planning, the scheme did not work until, in about 1890, a retired Naval petty officer was appointed; when not too heavily occupied, he helped out the Hall Porter. He was made Secretary of the Caddies Benefit Fund; this Fund was designed to help the families of regular caddies and to help those who, because of age or infirmity, could no longer carry. The Club gave generously to the Fund.

The North Berwick Golf Club appointed a Superintendent of

▷ *Littlestone Golf Club caddie badge. Without one a boy was not allowed to carry.*

△ *Cruden Bay Golf Club caddie badge. Only badge holders could carry and the* *badge could be taken away for bad behaviour.*

Caddies towards the end of the 19th century. A register of caddies was kept and those on the list had to wear arm badges, red for First Class caddies and blue for Second Class caddies. To be a First Class caddie you had to be over fourteen years of age and had to know the names of all the bunkers on the links. The fact that the Club ordered three hundred badges is some indication of the number of caddies

that were employed in those days.

In 1893, at Littlestone Golf Club in England efforts were made to regularise the hire of caddies. A tariff and some rules were posted in the Clubhouse. Each caddie had to have a badge and First Class caddies were to be paid two shillings and sixpence a round. 'Except on Saturdays and Public Holidays no caddie shall be employed unless he has reached the age of 13 years, or is exempted from attendance at School.' There was a Caddie Benefit Fund which paid out at Christmas and 'only badge boys and First Class Caddies shall be entitled to participate'.

The Club also introduced a system of 'black marks' for a variety of offences and decided that, at the Christmas shareout, caddies with no black marks would get three shares, those with one black mark two shares and those with two black marks one share. Caddies with three black marks would get nothing. The Superintendent of Caddies — and only through him could caddies be hired — was to keep a list of caddies and also a book in which were to be entered all black marks and the reason for them.

At Royal Wimbledon, in the latter part of the 19th century, only a few top professional caddies were employed. Boys were generally used and were graded into First Class and Second Class caddies. Each caddie had to have a caddie badge — and deposit sixpence against loss. The Club encouraged a caddie competition annually and gave prizes. Truancy from the local schools was a problem here, too. In 1920 Wimbledon caddies got a Christmas bonus and a new pair of boots, the latter were usually pawned to get more money. Later, a Caddies Benefit and Sickness Fund was started and mackintoshes were issued during bad weather.

The caddies got up to all sorts of tricks of which the most daring was to deceive the Prince of Wales, during his year of Captaincy, into believing that he had done a hole in one, in hopes of a fat tip. The caddies were fortunate in that there was one short hole where there was a bank which partially concealed the green from the tee. The trick worked, the Prince was very pleased and distributed large tips all round.

One of the old caddies at Wimbledon claimed that his master had a collie who used to walk round with them; the master gave the caddie twelve sheets of paper and instructed him to clean the collie's backside after he had 'done his business', for which the caddie was given an extra sixpence tip!

The Littlestone and Wimbledon arrangements were typical of English Golf Clubs at the end of the 19th century making an effort to discipline the caddies, regularise their employment and provide a bonus scheme for Christmas. It contrasts with the Scottish arrangements, which not only tried to achieve this but, in addition, tried to arrange long term benefits for the regular caddie who had made carrying a lifelong career. Such benefits were not necessary in England, as most caddies, however expert, regarded carrying as a means of earning a little extra money until a more permanent and lucrative

∇ *Royal Blackheath Golf Club, 1890. Black Heath Common was within 5 miles of St Paul's Cathedral. As the course was steadily encroached upon by park benches, lamp-posts, perambulators and walkers, so the caddies' duties became more difficult.*

job, unconnected with golf, should appear.

In the 1920s, at Beau Desert Golf Club, near Cannock, the Club photographed all its regular caddies. The pictures were all put in one frame and the picture (of twenty-four caddies) was hung on the wall of the Clubhouse. The idea of this 'rogues' gallery' was to enable golfers to identify a caddie who had carried for them and re-hire him — or vice versa if he was no good!

TRICKS OF THE TRADE

Despite all this help for the caddie, his rate of pay was low for the duties that he carried out. So, human nature being what it is, the more resourceful caddies found ways of improving their financial lot.

One way which they tried was to bet on the result of the game with the opposing caddie or caddies. This method was no more successful than backing horses — and for the same reason — the assessment of 'form' was very difficult. Although the caddie was fortunate, compared with the backer of horses, in that he knew that his 'horse' was trying; sometimes in golf the harder one tries the worse one plays. The caddie was therefore inclined to 'help' his master whenever he could, that is to say, whenever he felt himself safe from detection. These methods varied from quite blatant cheating, such as kicking the ball into a better lie in the rough, or 'finding' the ball in the rough by the simple expedient of dropping a ball of similar make and number down his trouser leg when all seemed lost. It was also quite possible, when indicating the line of a putt using a club, to select a point on the line where there was a rough patch and press firmly, thus reducing the roughness and making a slight groove where the rough patch had been. The Rules of Golf Committee saw through this one and issued an edict that no one may touch the line of a putt, except the player, and the latter may only use the weight of the putter to sweep the line of small, loose particles.

Other, slightly more subtle, methods were employed, such as coughing, sneezing, or dropping a club when the opposition was at the top of the backswing but, unless this was done with some skill, it might draw upon the caddie's head the wrath of both players.

More subtle, and probably equally effective, was to play upon the opponent's nerves. Horace Hutchinson, playing a hard match at North Berwick, was startled by his caddie saying, 'Come along then, Sir, step out, there is nothing puts Mr X (his opponent) off more than being hurried.'

Another ploy was giving misleading information in a loud voice. In the

19th century there was no such thing as a numbered set of clubs — all the clubs had names. The stage might well be set by the caddie by some such remark as 'I think the light iron for this one Sir', while handing his master the heavy iron. Darwin reports that on one occasion, on a foggy day and on a strange course, his opponent, aided by his caddie, took great care not to give him (Darwin) any indication as to what club he was using. In those days most iron clubs had 'Cleekmakers' marks on them, small symbols which were the trademark of the man who had made the iron head. The exchanges between Darwin's opponent and his caddie went something like this, 'I think this will be the pipe here, Sir' (the pipe was the trademark of Stewart of St Andrews) or, 'I think that I had better use the Bishop here, caddie' (a Bishop's Mitre was the trademark of Bishop and Hendry, who made iron clubs at Leith). As a result of this bit of gamesmanship Darwin found himself totally at a loss about which club to use.

The caddie was not averse, on occasions, to making some money at the expense of his master. A ball deep in the rough might be found by the caddie, who would put his foot on it in order to push it well into the ground; after the game, he would return to the spot, find the ball, and sell it to the professional. This system was known as 'dumping'. The dumper's style was somewhat cramped by the fact that he had to sell the ball to the professional, because it was a strict club rule that golfers must never buy balls found by caddies from them. The reason for this rule is self evident. Unfortunately, today's golfers are usually quite willing to do this and thus 'dumping' has become more prevalent than ever before. If the professional continually had balls brought to him by the same caddie, the latter might find himself banned from the course.

Mrs Williams, of Westward Ho! said that she was paid sixpence per round, with a deduction of threepence if a ball was lost; she found that the professional would pay ninepence for used balls. Thus, by losing a ball she could make an overall profit, so she 'dumped' with the best of them!

At St Andrews, when a ball went into the Swilken Burn, some caddies would plunge clubs in to look for it; this stirred up the mud enough so that the ball was not found — until later when the mud had settled.

▷ 'A sovereign for a ball.' In September each year the Captain elect of the Royal and Ancient Golf Club of St Andrews drives a ball from the first tee. When he has done this, he is Captain. The St Andrews' caddies wait down the fairway for the drive and he who picks the ball up and brings it to the new Captain is rewarded with a sovereign.

◁ *A Louis Wain cartoon of golfing cats and caddies. There are no golf balls in sight, but the lady has managed to break her club — perhaps in trying to kill one of the mice? One of them is disappearing down the hole from which the unusual flagstick with a spherical globe has been removed. Wain's obsession with cats was so marked as to be psychotic.*

Most caddies felt entitled to get away with anything that they could and beginners could be easy prey. A beginner bought a gutta golf ball from a caddie. After a few holes he noticed that the ball had 27 stamped on one side and 28 on the other (golf balls were stamped according to their weight in 'pennyweights'). When questioned about this, the caddie replied, 'Oh! you use the side marked 27 against the wind and the side marked 28 with the wind.'

Occasionally the caddie was caught out. Mr Chambers, of *Chambers Encyclopaedia*, had a caddie called Sweenum. One day Sweenum asked Chambers to lend him sixpence; Chambers had only two and sixpence on him. Sweenum offered to get him

▽ *A starting ball trough and a stand to raise the teebox, made by H. Pattisson and Co., 1910.*

▷ *The golfer has missed the ball and hit the ground. The caddie is clearly hoping to be given the club.*

Starting Ball Trough.

With the open Boards or Troughs in ordinary use, it is very easy for impatient caddies to manipulate the balls, and to secure an earlier start than they are entitled to. The "**Pattisson**" **Trough prevents this.** The first ball being inserted at the upper end runs to the bottom, and is followed by the succeeding balls in the order in which they have been put in, and it is impossible for this order to be interfered with until they reach the pocket at the bottom. The slot at the top is 1¼ inches wide, so that the balls are in full view and are quite distinguishable, but cannot be **lifted out.** On lifting the first ball all the others move down **automatically,** instead of having to be individually lifted and replaced, as is usually necessary. The Troughs are very strongly made of stout **Steel** plate, on Wrought Iron Frames, are **well galvanized after being made** and are painted with best Signal Red (or any other colour) Enamel. They will last a lifetime.

SECTION.

PRICE (3 feet long, holding 20 balls)	...	...	...	Low Stand, **10/-** each.
,, ,, ,, ,, ,,	...	...	...	High Stand, **12/6** ,,
,, (4 feet, 6 inches long, holding 30 balls)	...	...	...	Low Stand, **12/6** ,,
,, ,, ,, ,, ,,	...	...	...	High Stand, **15/-** ,,

Wood Trough.

WOOD TROUGHS, substantially made and well painted, holding 20 balls, **7/6** ,,

WOOD BENCHES, ,, ,, ,, ,, 30 ,, **8/6** ,,

SPIRAL BALL TUBE, ,, ,, Galvanized, ,, 20 ,, **7/-** ,,

(The Tube can be hung on a fence or post in a convenient position).

THE RESULT OF HIS EFFORTS.

change and went off with the half crown, which he proceeded to spend at the local pub and then went home. Sweenum kept well away for a few weeks and was surprised, on his return, when Chambers asked him to carry for him. At the end of the round Chambers said to Sweenum, 'Do you remember the half a crown that I gave you? Well, now we are quits.'

Sometimes fraud was practised on a grander scale; there are two old wooden putters in existence, both of which are said to be the putter with which Willie Park Senior won the first Open Championship in 1860; one even has a silver plate on which the donor (in all innocence) makes this statement. The stamp on the head of the club is indistinct but 'W' can be seen and also an 'A', as well as what could be an 'R'. With a powerful lens it can be seen that the name is, in fact, W. Watt, a fine clubmaker — but born in 1867!

On one occasion at North Berwick three visitors from overseas were going to play a round; they were accompanied by a fourth man, who did not play golf. During the morning round the fourth man poured scorn and contempt on the game, which he described as silly and only suitable for children. After a good lunch, his three friends persuaded him to try to play. One of the caddies, who had heard his disparaging comments during the morning, offered to get him a set of clubs to play with; the set that the caddie produced comprised half right-handed clubs and half left-handed clubs. The man recognised that something was wrong and said indignantly to the caddie, 'Do you think I am a fool? Some of these clubs are the wrong way round!' to which the caddie replied, 'Not at all, sir, you are supposed to use the right-handed clubs on the outward nine and the left-handed clubs on the second nine.'

Occasionally caddies scored because they did not have to do a full round but might be paid a full wage. In this respect one caddie did particularly well. He carried for a stockbroker at Walton Heath; the player had never had a lesson and knew little about the game. He would arrive from the City when the course was quiet, change his coat and then proceed to the first tee in 'pin stripe' trousers. He would hack his way down the first hole and continue to play until he got into a bunker; he would then get his niblick out and hack the ball in the bunker. He never managed to get his ball out but, when he considered that he had had enough exercise, he would throw down the club and return to the Clubhouse.

Others were less fortunate, one caddie had a master who was a very bad golfer and also very bad tempered. He would hack at the ball, taking a large divot, and then throw the club down in disgust and walk on to the next shot. His caddie would have none of this and eventually said, 'No! No! I will put the divot back and you can pick up the club, or you can put the divot back and I will pick up the club, but I am not doing both!'

Despite all these tricks and difficulties, there was a bond of loyalty between a professional caddie and his regular employer. The term 'we' epitomises the bond. All the professional caddies used this term when talking of the game; it was always 'We played badly', 'We missed a short putt at the tenth', etc. The caddie genuinely wanted his master to do well and this was not just because he had a bet on the game. In fact, a professional caddie would extend all his help to anybody for whom he carried, providing his master was willing to try and, particularly, if he had some skill at the game. He would flatter him, if this would help, or pour scorn on him when he played badly, if the caddie thought that this would make his master play better; he was quite willing to teach him on the way round, telling him what he was doing wrong. It is said that one golfer, with a regular caddie, had a besetting sin of swinging back too fast. The caddie was instructed to say to his master,

▷ *What a predicament! If the player plays the ball he will probably break his club. The* *caddie looks interested but clearly can offer no solution. Cartoon by John Hassall, c. 1910.*

before every shot, 'Slow back'. This went on for many years until his master died. The caddie then carried for other golfers, but the habit would not die, he irritated many golfers thereafter by intoning 'Slow back' every time he gave them a club.

The era from 1800 to 1900 might be termed the golden age of the professional caddie, as far as amateur golf was concerned, but changes were taking place which would alter the trade of carrying clubs considerably. Before looking into this, let us consider some of the great characters among the caddies of that age.

TO MY CADDIE.

" Persicos odi, puer, apparatus."—*Horat. Carm. i. 38.*

"I HATE GREAT SHOW OF APPARATUS."

I will not overload thee, boy !
I hate great show of apparatus :
Whilst I'm at 10 I'll still enjoy
My lowly status.

My brassie, iron, mashie, cleek,
For present wants I find sufficient :
Some small additions I may seek
When more proficient.

Some day, perhaps, when I'm at scratch,
You'll find my choice far more specific :
Ten clubs at least for every match—
A weight terrific !

Meanwhile, I do not care to spoil
Our tempers yet by turning faddy :
A game shall not be made a toil
For self or caddie.

P.S.W.

CHARACTERS

The very names of these early caddies suggest that they were men of character: 'Big' Crawford, 'Fiery' John Carey, Old Da', Lang Willie, Sandy Smith, Tweedly, Sweenum, Donald Blue, 'Skipper', 'Poot' Chisholm, 'Pawky' Corstorphine. For the most part these men came from Musselburgh, North Berwick and St Andrews. Their names have gone down in caddie folklore and the tales of them have been repeated and embellished so often that they are now, largely, apocryphal. There must

◁ *An illustrated* Ode to my caddie, *1910. The tripod bag-stand is a new invention.*

▷*John Carey of Musselburgh was a famous caddie in the 1890s. His nickname 'Fiery' stemmed not from his temperament but from his complexion, which was copper coloured. He was a quiet taciturn man, whose excellent advice was only given when asked for. He was the regular caddie of Willie Park Junior in all his big matches and tournaments and the two made a formidable team. 'Fiery' invariably wore a 'Balmoral' bonnet. Having begun carrying long before the advent of golf bags, he continued to carry clubs and bag under his arm.*

have been many more caddies, at Prestwick, Dornoch, Carnoustie and all the other links in Scotland, but they have not come to notice in the wider world and remain as local — and often unsung — heroes.

Space does not permit a detailed biography of them all, but a few anecdotes will indicate what rugged individualists they were.

'Big' Crawford

'Big' Crawford was a huge man, with a fog horn of a voice, who was a caddie at North Berwick and Musselburgh. In his early days he had been a playing professional, so he was very knowledgeable about the game and how to play it.

He persuaded the North Berwick Golf Club to allow him to set up a ginger beer stall at about the half-way stage on the links where he would preside when not otherwise engaged. 'Big' Crawford was a regular caddie of Mr A. J. Balfour. Both men developed an affection for each other and treated one another as equals. When Balfour won a competition he always gave Crawford the money that he had won in the sweepstake. In later years, when Crawford ran the ginger beer stall and only carried occasionally, he would enquire of the early competitors whether 'Arthur' was playing? If he was, Crawford would run up a small flag on his stall in his honour.

It is said that on one occasion both 'Arthur' and the Grand Duke Michael of Russia were playing; when the Duke arrived at the stall, he noticed the flag and thanked Crawford for honouring him, to which Crawford replied that the flag was not raised for foreigners but only for Mr Balfour.

Crawford's other master was Ben Sayers, a great tournament professional, and a club-maker at North Berwick. The two made an interesting physical contrast, as Crawford was a very large man and Ben Sayers was small. Sayers had been an acrobat in a circus in his youth and was small and wiry; it was not unknown for him, on holing a particularly important putt, to do an impromptu hand spring.

On one occasion, in a very important money match, a mushroom was found on the green in the line of Sayers' putt. Crawford removed it, saying that it was dead, but Sayers' opponent claimed that it had been growing and therefore should not have been removed, and claimed the hole. An argument ensued in which Crawford's giant physical presence and fog horn voice predominated. At length, Crawford, driven to exasperation, pronounced, 'Weel, het's the rule of the game an—', pausing to raise a fist like a leg of mutton, 'this is the referee!' Needless to say there was no further argument.

△ *'Big Crawford' sitting at his ginger beer stall on North Berwick Golf Links. His face shows him to be a man of decided opinions — and not to be trifled with! As he is seated, his large size is not evident.*

◁ *Portrait of an old caddie. Of serious mien, he is a proud professional, of the era when clubs were carried under the arm. His cloth cap with a shiny peak was common head gear for working men in his time, and was known as a 'cheesecutter'.*

▷ Sandy Smith, a great caddie of the 'old school' in the North Berwick area. He was renowned for his caustic wit — and for his drinking. He told everybody at North Berwick that the finest golfer in the area was Mr Edward Blyth. He was asked, when in his cups, 'Why?' and he replied 'Well, his clothes fit me very well!'

▷ David Duff. He appears to be rather grim, but he was a good professional caddie and had a fund of stories. He carried once for an old gentleman who played in 'patent leather' shoes and wore a velvet jacket and white cuffs. He kept a snuff box in his waistcoat pocket which he filled with sand from the nearest bunker, using a teaspoon, and taking exaggerated care not to get sand on his fingers or cuffs. When he got to the tee, he removed the sand from the snuff box, using the teaspoon to make the tee.

Bill Marr

Bill Marr, another North Berwick caddie, had a rich 'regular' who was a smart dresser; consequently, Marr was the best dressed caddie at North Berwick. Marr was a very heavy drinker and was frequently paralytically drunk after lunch. In the afternoon he sometimes staggered as far as the 'Quarry' hole but was prone to slide down the slope and go to sleep, leaving his master to carry his own clubs.

Lang Willie

Lang Willie was a St Andrews caddie and frequently carried for members of the University staff. He was a tall, rather lugubrious individual who insisted, if asked, that he only drank sweet milk but was, nevertheless, regularly found to be drunk. His normal attire was a tall hat, swallow-tail coat and light trousers, all extremely dirty.

The standard of golf among the University intelligentsia was a source

of great disappointment to him and he is reputed to have expressed the view to the other caddies that 'Learning Latin and Greek was all very fine but you need brains to be a golfer.'

Occasionally Lang Willie would accompany a particular member of the University staff when he went to practise. The latter was a very poor golfer, who, at his very best, only hit the ball a short distance but was so short-sighted that he could not see the ball. Willie would tee up a number of balls for him and comment on his drives with remarks such as 'Eh! but that's a maist awfu' drive' or, 'Guid save us, saw a body iver the like o' that'. Unknown to the player, Willie had sent a small boy ahead whose job was to pick up the balls, carry them on another fifty yards and then drop them. When Willie got bored, he would advise his master that he had had enough and must not go on lest he get stale; he would then lead his master down to pick up the balls. His master would be very pleased that he was driving much further than usual and declare to all that Willie was a most invaluable caddie and had much improved his driving.

Old Da'

Old Da', as David Anderson was known, was a caddie and a greenkeeper in the very old days of golf at St Andrews. When he retired he, like Crawford, was allowed to run a ginger beer stall, this one being at the ninth hole on the Old Course. He was a great character with a ready wit. He had four sons, all of whom became professional golfers; one of them, James, won the Open Championship three years in succession, 1877, '78, '79. Unfortunately, to win the Open was not the crock of gold that it is now and James died in complete poverty in the workhouse near Perth.

Donald Blue

Donald Blue was a St Andrews caddie who knew all about golf. On one occasion he carried for a man who was very anxious to win an important match. Donald said, 'Leave it to me, I'll tell ye what to play and what to do.' At the 16th hole his master left a chip woefully short; Donald decided

▷ *Old Da' at his ginger beer stall. David Anderson was a greenkeeper at St Andrews in about 1850. Later in life he took to carrying and, when he retired from that, he was allowed to run a ginger beer stall at the 9th hole on the Old Course. Most of the famous golfers of the day had a drink at his stall at one time or another, and Old Tom Morris was a regular visitor. Old Da' was wont to bewail, in his later years, the loss of the whins at St Andrews which, in the old days, made the Old Course so narrow and difficult.*

◁ *Donald Blue or Blae, a 'character' among the St Andrews' caddies in the late 19th century. He and another caddie, Archie Stump, held an annual fun match for £5. They put on an uproarious show which attracted a gallery of 300-400. All the other caddies threw divots at them and, at the end, they were both ducked in the Swilken Burn. Despite his capers, he was a shrewd caddie.*

▷ *Bob Martin was caddie, player and Open Champion in 1876 and 1885. In the 1876 Open another player, David Strath, had to do the last two holes in 10 in order to tie. He did, but when hitting a long second at the 17th put the ball on to the green when the players in front were still putting. This breached a then Rule of Golf and another player tried to disqualify him. After a row, he was awarded the tie, but refused to play off.*

that the next shot had better be a run-up shot. He gave him the club, and then gave him a line several yards to the right of the hole. The player demurred over the line, to which Donald replied, 'Yours no' to reason why, yours juist to do what y'ere bluidy well telt!'

5. THE CADDIE STORY
SINCE 1900

In order to appreciate the changes in the employment and distribution of caddies in the United Kingdom, the reader should be aware of the changes in golf between 1840 and 1900.

GOLF BECOMES A POPULAR SPORT

Until 1848, when the gutta golf ball was introduced, golf had been for fifty or sixty years a rich man's game. With the advent of the gutta ball, people of lower income groups could afford to play, and were aided in this by the country's increasing industrialisation and its accompanying legislation which limited working hours and introduced the idea of annual holidays.

Golf ceased to be the exclusive sport of the rich and was open to all. The result was a golf explosion: in 1800 there were 7 Golf Clubs in the UK, in 1850 there were 17, in 1900 there were 2,330 and, by 1910, 4,135.

In order to supply all these extra golfers with clubs and balls, mass production was introduced. The craftsmen club-makers went out of business, gutta golf balls were, likewise, mass produced. The keeper of the green became the club professional and a specialist greenkeeper looked after the course.

At first sight, this explosion could be expected to lead to a very much increased demand for caddies, but it did not work out like that. Many of the new golfers were not rich and did not wish to afford a caddie; there was a much higher percentage of inexpert golfers, who, if they did employ a caddie, saw no point in employing a professional caddie but were content with a young boy who was just a bag carrier and, therefore, cheaper.

Although a nucleus of professional caddies remained, the numbers were dwindling, partly because of lack of demand but, also, because an increasingly affluent society could earn much better money in other jobs, making carrying as a life-time profession less attractive. In Scotland the traditional areas of golf continued to produce good caddies but, in the rest of the UK where, in general, there was no such tradition, most of the

▷ *A 1912 advertisement for the Wood Milne golf ball.*

The company made rubbercore golf balls in Preston, Lancashire.

72

caddies were schoolboys trying to earn a little extra pocket money; they had no intention of going on to become adult professional caddies. Outside Scotland and a small number of English clubs, such as Blackheath, Westward Ho!, Sunningdale, Royal St George's at Sandwich and Hoylake, a well trained caddie became a relic of the past.

Although there might be as many as thirty to forty caddies at a club, they were mostly schoolboys. In time the numbers of schoolboys was reduced as implementation of the Truancy Acts was more strictly enforced. A further blow came when, in 1912, new National Insurance regulations meant that every boy over sixteen had to have a National Insurance stamp.

◁ A group on the first tee at Westward Ho! in 1925. On the left is the starter, who is Charles Gibson, club professional and master club-maker. One of the players has his chauffeur carrying for him.

▷ A very tall golfer and a very small caddie photographed at North Berwick. The picture was intended to underline the effect of the Insurance Act of 1912 by which caddies over the age of 16 were compelled to be insured, so it was cheaper to employ very young caddies.

Some Golf Clubs made an effort to train a new generation of caddies; Walton Heath Golf Club is a case in point. In 1914, the Club decided that, in the slack season, which in that area was the summer when many members were away on holiday, they would send some of their caddies to selected clubs on the South coast, or even to Scotland, with fares paid and a guaranteed wage, to train them. Unfortunately, the outbreak of the First World War meant that this scheme was never put into effect.

The changes wrought by the huge increases in golfers and the various regulations concerning the employment of young boys had least effect in Scotland. The Scots had a long tradition of golf and the links were very close to villages. Schoolboys, living right on the links, played golf with one club on any piece of flat land and were passionately interested in the game. The elderly and retired still had time to lean on a fence, smoke a pipe and criticise the passing golfers; talk in the home was of golfers and golfing. Small boys still crowded around the first tee with shrill cries of 'Carry your bag, Sir?', and were paid sixpence or a shilling a round. Older boys, more experienced and better dressed, often wearing both shoes and stockings, waited respectfully for the better players and, when hired, took over the management of the game for those who were visitors, determined

that 'we' were going to play our best. As one small caddie said to a visitor waiting his turn to get on the tee, 'Dinna stand there daein' nothing, get awa' owre there and practise yer swing.' On another occasion, having handed the player an iron for his second shot and he being at the top of the backswing, 'Stoap! Stoap I havena' decided yet whether we will use the wood!'

THE FIRST WORLD WAR

When the First World War came, caddies joined up. Such was the loyalty owed them by the club that many continued to be paid five shillings a week throughout the war. Golf magazines published letters from golfers urging fellow golfers not to employ anybody over the age of sixteen who was fit, as they should be joining up. Some caddies, believing that, as they were in the habit of carrying about sixteen pounds of golf clubs ten to twelve miles a day, they must be fit, were dismayed to be turned down for the Forces because they had flat feet.

▷ *Golfing cartoon, 1911. 'Something really good at the next tee,' A topped tee shot was always the fault of the caddie for making the sand tee too low. If you told the caddie this, you could expect something really good at the next tee.*

After the War conditions changed yet again. There was much unemployment and many semi-disabled ex-soldiers. Golf Clubs encouraged them to carry clubs; this meant that fewer small boys were employed and could really only be certain of any employment at weekends. These changes were mainly felt in England. In Scotland, the professional caddie could still find employment, though the numbers were dwindling as fewer new caddies were recruited than those who had to give up.

▽ 'Hollis', a caddie at Beau Desert Golf Club in Staffordshire in the 1920s and a disabled soldier from the First World War. He cycled to work on his fixed wheel bicycle with his crutches strapped to the cross bar and then, regularly, carried for 36 holes in a day, although the Club forbade him to go on the greens.

▽ 'Sergeant' Hickman. Another veteran from the First World War who carried at Beau Desert Golf Club. He was a stickler for discipline.

These two caddies, and the 22 others, had their photographs pasted up in the Clubhouse. Visitors could select — or avoid — the caddie that they had had on the last occasion!

Golf Flags and Staffs.

The Staffs (excepting Figs. 5, 5A, 5B, 5C, 6 and 9, which are solid) are made of **wrought iron tubing, combining lightness with great strength,** and are **Indestructible.** All Staffs are supplied with pointed or blunt ends, as desired.

In **Fig. 1** the Bunting or Cotton Flag is inserted in a slot at the top of the Staff, and is secured by a brass screw cap, so that it **cannot possibly come off** accidentally. The dirty flags can be exchanged for clean ones without removing the staff from the tin. This is an **extremely neat and effective staff,** and **one which cannot be worn out.**

In Figs. 2, 3, 5, 5A, 5B, 5C and 7, the Flags are made of Strong **Steel** plates **(galvanized), not tin, or zinc,** painted with best White or Red Enamel, or any colour desired.

Fig. 3 is a Balloon-shaped Flag. It is very strong and light, being made of **Steel plate** (galvanized); the staff passes through it, and is secured by a brass screw cap. Well painted in Red or White Enamel, or in 2 colours, if preferred. **Very effective.**

Fig. 4 allows the Bunting or Cotton Flag to revolve with the wind.

NEW STEEL FLAGS. The Special Feature of Figs. 2 and 7, Revolving Flags, is that they are so constructed that on being lifted from the Tin, **they can be placed on the Green upside down on the wings, without the slightest damage to the grass, as shown below.**

PRACTICE PUTTING-GREEN FLAGS. Figs. 5, 5A, and 5C are made 18 inches or 2 feet high for this purpose at very moderate prices. See below. These Flags are **the most suitable for use on Lawns.**

Fig. 9 is a Wrought Iron Staff, with best Worsted Tassel.

WICKER-WORK BALLOON FLAGS. A new balloon-shaped flag made of strong wicker-work has been introduced, the special advantage claimed for this device being **its lightness** as compared with steel balloons as per Fig. 3 below. In consequence of this greater lightness **a much larger balloon can be used,** which is **conspicuous at a greater distance from the hole.**

EXTRA LIGHT TUBULAR STEEL FLAG STAFFS. As per Fig. 10. Of great strength and Indestructible. This is a finely finished Staff, and is strongly recommended where a specially light Staff, combined with great strength and durability, is required. It cannot damage the green by being thrown down.

SPRING STEEL STAFFS (Fig. 8). Special attention is drawn to these Staffs, which, being made of **Spring Steel,** are very light and resilient, "giving" to the wind but always returning to the upright. They will last a lifetime and are strongly recommended as most satisfactory in use.

ALL STAFFS SUPPLIED WITH BLUNT SPIKES, IF DESIRED.

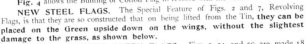

FIG. 1.   FIG. 2.   FIG. 5.   FIG. 5A.   FIG. 5B.   FIG. 5C.

PRICES.

Fig. 1, Tubular Wrought Iron Staff, 4 feet or under, with Bunting Flag	**2/6** each.
„ 2, Three Wing Steel Flags, 4 feet or under ...	**3/0** „
„ 7, Four-Wing „ „ ...	**3/0** „
„ 3, Balloon Steel Flags, 4 feet or under	**5/0** „
„ 4, Tubular Wrought Iron Staff with Cotton Flag, 4 feet or under, Revolving	**2/0** „
„ 5, 5A, 5B, 5C, Wrought Iron Staffs with Numbered Steel Flags, 4 feet high, **2/0**; 3 feet, **1/9**; 18 inches ...	**1/6** „
„ 5C, Smaller Flags, 18 inches ... **1/0** each.
„ 6, Wrought Iron Staffs (with Cotton Flags), 3 feet high	**1/3** „
„ 8, **Spring-Steel Staffs** with Bunting Flags, 4 feet ...	**4/-** „
„ 9, Wrought Iron Staff with Tassel, 4 feet ...	**1/9** „
„ 10, **Tubular Steel Staff** with Bunting Flag, 4 feet ...	**2/6** „
Wicker Balloons Painted any Colour with best Bamboo Staff, 6 feet	**5/0** „

The above Flagstaffs of **any extra height** at per foot (or part) **3d.,** excepting Figs. 5, 5A, 5B, 5C, 6 and 9, which are **2d.,** only per extra foot.

FIG. 3.   FIG. 7.   FIG. 7 on the green.   FIG. 8.

THE RISE OF THE PROFESSIONAL

At this time, further changes in the golfing scene meant a better carrying job for the small band of professional caddies that remained. The beginnings of a professional golf 'circuit' had started; there were more professional tournaments and the prize money was rising. The great players of the turn of the century, such as Vardon, Braid, Taylor, Herd and Ray, had all been able to make an adequate living out of playing golf; they were now able to make an even better living and it paid them to hire a caddie who knew something of their game and who had a good local knowledge of the course on which the tournament was to be played. To achieve this, they were willing to pay well over the usual caddie fee and to slip the caddie extra money if they won.

After the War the Americans, who had an even more lucrative tournament circuit in their own country, came over to try conclusions with the British professionals; because

British golf courses were very different from those in the USA it was even more important for them to have a good caddie and they were prepared to pay. As far as the caddies were concerned, it was a good start, but although only a few could benefit it was an augury of things to come. Already some caddies were required to travel with their employers to courses other than their own local ones because the golfer felt comfortable with a man who knew his game and whose considerable experience would enable him to 'read' satisfactorily even those courses that he had not seen before.

In the 1920s and 1930s regular caddies thought nothing of walking to the local course for a job. As a boy the author can remember that the caddies walked about two and a half miles to the course, along the beach if the tide were low, or along the cliff top at high tide. This meant that, if the caddie were fortunate enough to carry for two rounds, he would walk about seventeen miles in the day, for twelve of which he would have carried a bag of clubs weighing about sixteen pounds.

In 1920, caddies walked from London to Deal, a distance of eighty miles, sleeping rough on the way, in order to carry in the Open Championship being played at Royal Cinque Ports Golf Club. Some players and spectators were so impressed that

◁ *This cartoon by Charles Ambrose in 1928 is entitled 'The Cultured Caddie'. It stemmed from a report in the American press that it was becoming common in America for* *well-educated people to carry on the US tournament circuit in order to earn extra money. The cartoonist envisages the caddie reading hints on how to play to his master.*

△ *Part of a band of caddies, some invalided out of the armed forces at the end of the war, who walked from London to Deal for the 1920 Open Championship in the hope of a carrying job. They did well and spectators subscribed to a fund which raised enough money to send them back to London by train.*

they had a whip round and gave all the caddies their fares back to London at the end of the Championship.

As a result of all these changes the schoolboy caddie, even in Scotland, was less in evidence. He had to work harder at school and many players either could not afford his services or were prepared to do without him. Instead of the club caddie master having to turn away boy caddies at the weekend, only a few put in an appearance and they did not always find employment.

▷ *An unknown group of golfers, 1920. Their jerseys suggest that they are fishermen. Probably, when not fishing or playing golf, they carried, an occupation that the fishermen of St Andrews referred to as 'grass hoppin'' or 'working on the land'. There are only three golf bags, possibly they shared the golf clubs.*

PROFESSIONAL PLAYERS
AND PROFESSIONAL CADDIES

The dwindling number of caddies led
to changes in the supply of
professional players. Before the First
World War, all professional players
had previously been professional
caddies. The great amateur players
remained amateurs; had this state of
affairs continued, the number of
professional golfers would have
dwindled. After the War, good artisan
golfers entered the professional ranks
as they discovered that they could
earn more money at golf than they
could at their usual employment. This
helped to maintain the numbers, and
the ranks of the professional
tournament players were further
augmented by the addition of talented
amateur golfers who had never been
caddies.

From the artisan clubs came Abe
Mitchell who had been beaten in the
final of the Amateur Championship at
Westward Ho! in 1912 and had then
become a professional.

John Henry Taylor, a caddie golfer
if ever there was one, also came from a
poor family. When he became a
famous professional, he championed
the cause of the golfer who was not
rich. He was a great, and articulate,
supporter of artisan clubs and public
courses. He, in particular, encouraged
a proper standard of dress and
behaviour both on and off the course
and set standards which many of
today's professionals could adopt
with advantage.

After the First World War, Henry
Cotton appeared on the scene. A
talented teenage player, he came from
a middle class background, had never
known real poverty and certainly

never carried clubs for a living. Although Taylor and his generation of professionals had grumbled that they were not adequately paid for their services, their complaints were somewhat negative. When Cotton became a successful professional, he took an immediate and positive attitude by asking a great deal more money for his services than had ever before been considered – and got it. Thus he built on Taylor's foundation of proper dress and behaviour, giving status to the professional, by insisting that a professional was worth a good fee.

As far as the British professional was concerned, Cotton was instrumental in raising his financial status, a status which, with the advent of television and 'media hype' has now gone 'over the top'. Despite the good that this did to his brother professionals, the 'old guard' did not like it and there was much bitterness and jealousy – but that is another story.

A solid nucleus of professional caddies remained in Scotland and their expertise in Scottish golf began to pay off, both in professional and in major amateur events. This was very noticeable in the Open, mainly because about four out of six Open Championships were played in Scotland. Bobbie Cruikshank had Willie Black of St Andrews as a caddie in the Open of 1929. After a tee shot

at the first hole he asked Black for a No. 2 iron for the second shot. Black responded, '*I'll* give you the club, *you* play the bloody shot!'

Regular professional caddies in England now began to find it worth their while to sell their own expertise. When Sarazen won the Open at Sandwich in 1932 he was so impressed with the help given him by his caddie that he asked if the caddie could come up on the platform with him when he received the cup.

Henry Cotton paid a handsome tribute to Ernest Butler, his caddie at Sandwich, who caddied for him in both the Open Championships that Cotton won in 1934 and 1937. Butler, one of the First World War veterans, was invalided out of the Army; he eked out his pension by carrying at Sandwich, his local course. Recommended to Cotton by the local professional, he was a tower of strength. He knew the links well and was very knowledgeable about the greens. Not only did he 'club' Cotton well but he knew the lines of the putts so that Cotton, after a few holes, gave up trying to read the putts and simply left Butler to tell him the exact line to take.

When Tony Lema won the Open at St Andrews in 1964 he had had only two practice rounds on a links that he had never seen before and, moreover, a links which has more 'local knowledge' than almost any other!

He employed 'Tip' Anderson as his caddie and it was Tip's local knowledge and expertise, combined with Lema's ability to hit the shots required of him, that gave him an easy win. Lema freely admitted afterwards that without his caddie he could not have won.

The dominant role taken by Anderson in helping Lema brings up the interesting question of the dominance of the player, or his caddie, in any 'team' effort on the course. Some players are irritated by too much advice and prefer to have a small lad, provided he keeps quiet, who sees where the ball goes and

△ Henry Cotton playing at Walton Heath in 1937. On the left is Cotton's caddie, Ernest Butler. Butler carried for Cotton in many tournaments and, particularly, in the Open Championships of 1934 and 1937, which Cotton won; Butler also carried for Cotton in the 1937 Ryder Cup Match. Here Butler is carrying for Cotton in a 72-hole match against Densmore

Shute. Shute, originally from Devon, was US PGA Champion in 1937 and had previously won the Open Championship in 1933. Cotton beat him by 6 and 5.

Cotton liked Butler because he was imperturbable and quite undisturbed by large galleries. He never offered advice unless asked for it and was a master at reading the line to the hole on the green.

speaks only if spoken to. Bernard Darwin and Henry Longhurst were of this type of player, preferring to make their own mistakes; both became very irritated, for instance, if the caddie pulled a club out of the bag before the player asked for it. Gratuitous advice on the line of a putt they also found disturbing. They preferred boy caddies for this reason; as Sir Walter Simpson had said many years before, 'Boys are more scoldable'; one did not scold a professional adult caddie at St Andrews without getting a pretty sharp reply! Henry Longhurst points out that the boy caddie is a very useful alibi for playing bad golf, 'That wretched boy!' could be made responsible for much bad golf. Cotton and Lema, however, were clearly glad to be rid of the pressure of judging distance and line, and allowed the caddie to take this pressure off them, thus leaving them to concentrate solely on the problem of striking the ball properly. It is the satisfactory adjustment of problems of this sort that will make or break a golfer/caddie partnership.

I once played against the late Leonard Crawley in a National Championship and was confronted with a formidable partnership in which the caddie entirely dominated the team. Crawley was a great golfer and, in fact, a great all round ball game player. On the first tee he was

sportsmanlike but decisive and said that he had no wish to upset my game and warned that he did not watch his opponent's shots. Indeed, he studiously looked in the other direction whenever a shot through the green was played. This was not upsetting, nor was it intended to be. His invariable caddie was Ron Mullins, a very experienced professional from Sunningdale — and a great character. The progress of the game went something like this: After Crawley had been given the best line off the tee by Mullins, he drove off. When the second shot was due, Mullins handed him a club and made a sign with his right hand; he would either turn the palm of the hand upward, or downward. If turned upward, this meant that the shot was to be faded from left to right; if downward, the shot was to be played with draw, from right to left. If no sign was made this meant, of course, that a straight shot was required. When the green was reached, Mullins would hand Crawley a putter and then study the line; he would then take the pin and point with a club to the exact spot at which Crawley was to aim, concluding with some such words as, 'Slightly downhill and fairly fast', or whatever seemed helpful.

The system worked admirably and Crawley, taking care not to see my shots, did exactly as ordered by

Mullins and won a good match. It was clear that he wished to play against 'par' and preferred not to know what his opponent was doing; he also wished to concentrate solely on hitting the ball properly, as ordered. It was an interesting experience; in retrospect, I have thought that 'nobbling' Mullins during the night might have altered the result, but this is probably just wishful thinking.

△ *Ron Mullins. Always a snappy dresser, he appears in this photograph in front of the Clubhouse at Sunningdale, rather better dressed than most of the members. Mullins was not only a great caddie but, also, a natural comedian. At* one time he carried for H. M. Tennant of theatrical fame; Tennant thought he could make a good living as a professional comedian and tried to persuade him to go on the stage, but Mullins preferred the open-air life of a caddie.

OUR NEW PRO
HITS A
"SCREAMER"

▷ *Francis Ouimet and his caddie Eddie Lowry in 1913. When Harry Vardon and Edward Ray went to America on tour in 1913, it was assumed that one of them was bound to win the US Open Championship. To everyone's surprise Francis Ouimet, a local, 17-year-old amateur, not only tied with them but then beat them in a play off.*

Ten-year-old Eddie Lowry carried for Ouimet throughout the Championship even though, when it came to the tie, he was offered money to let others carry. The Americans thought that caddies were small boys who knew little about golf, so they did not value any particular caddie, nor seek his advice. When Ouimet was told that Eddie Lowry was being offered money not to carry in the tie, he said that it was up to Eddie to decide; he did not value Lowry's services enough to persuade him to continue to carry for him.

△ *Menu card for the West Middlesex Golf Club's Annual dinner, 1901. The decoration of this menu card was done by Hal Ludlow, a well-known artist and sculptor. Ludlow, a fine golfer, had represented Wales in the Home Internationals. His bronze of Harry Vardon is the best of the statuettes of the great man.*

As a young lad, in 1913, Francis Ouimet, of the US, tied for the US Open with Vardon and Ray; as Ouimet was an amateur and Vardon and Ray were the two best professionals in the world at that time, this was a remarkable achievement and Ouimet followed it up by winning the play-off. He had a ten-year-old boy carrying for him. According to the account, the boy, Eddie Lowry, often told him to keep his eye on the ball, but there is no account of any other advice. It is

△ 'A Desirable Member' and, in fact, an advertisement for Buchanan-Walker whisky. The player wears 'plus-fours', a form of dress made popular by the Prince of Wales. The caddie wears some patched trousers and a 'cheesecutter' cap.

unlikely that a ten-year-old would be experienced enough to give much advice – other than the very fundamental and useful advice which he is said to have repeated. The story suggests that Ouimet was of the same opinion as Darwin and Longhurst in preferring a willing lad to an adult professional who might well upset his concentration by offering unwanted, if well meaning, advice.

One suspects that Bobby Jones was in the same camp as in his own account of the Open Championship he does not even name his caddie, who, he says, was a pleasant lad of about twenty and who said to Jones at one stage, 'You are a wonder, Sir!', for which compliment Jones laughed and patted him on the back. It certainly does not sound as if Jones had long and anxious consultations with him on what club to play, or on the line of a putt.

THE DECLINE OF THE CADDIE

The situation of boy caddies after the Second World War became even more precarious; the 'caddie cart' made its appearance and this virtually put them out of business. Only a relatively few boys in Scotland got jobs and this mainly carrying for visitors in the summer holidays.

Few adult caddies can now make a living, except at the popular links in Scotland, such as St Andrews, where something like a hundred thousand visitors play annually. Many of them are used to 'buggies' and, in any event have long since forgotten what it is like to carry their own clubs; as carts and buggies are not allowed on the Old Course, they have, perforce, to take a caddy. A similar situation obtains at Muirfield, except that Muirfield would not allow a hundred thousand golfers on its course in a year. Some of the London courses have a small nucleus of caddies but, as far as amateur, everyday, golf is concerned, carrying clubs is a thing of the past.

On the professional golf circuit, a caddie is a well paid and important person; if a good caddie, with whom you can form a satisfactory partnership, can help you win a five figure sum of money, you are prepared to pay him well, including a retainer for his services when he is not actually carrying. Thus the age old partnership of golfer and caddie survives, a rich harvest for the caddie – but only for the few.

6. CADDIES ABROAD

△ Caddies at Colombo in Ceylon (as it then was), 1901. The Club had both British and local (coloured) members.

From the mid 19th century golf was played outside the United Kingdom. Indeed, it is clear that golf was played in America in the 18th century, but there are no specific, detailed records as to how it was played.

Not surprisingly, most golf was played in the British Empire and played by the mad Scots and, almost as mad, English. The local inhabitants were very tolerant and even helped them to do it, but showed no inclination to join in.

THE INDIAN SUBCONTINENT

The earliest of these golfing areas was the Indian subcontinent, probably because the British were more numerous in this area of the Empire than in any other. Golf Clubs were founded at Calcutta in 1832, Bombay in 1842 and Colombo in 1879.

Little is known about caddies in the early days of golf on the Indian subcontinent, but they certainly existed. In the Indian Empire servants were not a luxury to the European,

△ *The Clubhouse of Kingston and St Andrews Golf Club,* *Jamaica, 1901. The caddies were also excellent golfers.*

they were a necessity; each household had many of them. Caddies would have been a further extension of the army of servants and so perhaps not worthy of mention.

In the official history of the Royal Calcutta Golf Club, the first mention of caddies is in 1909 when it seems that there were forty registered caddies and a Caddie Master was appointed. The caddies were paid three annas per round of nine holes. Why was there no mention of caddies before this time? A possible answer was that, in the early days, each golfer brought one of his servants to act as a caddie and that it was only after many years that golfers came to hire a caddie on arrival at the Club.

The first mention of caddies at the Royal Colombo Golf Club was in 1900, when they went on strike for more money. Eventually, they got their way and the strike ended. A member at that time suggested that, if they wanted more money they should become better caddies and proposed a catechism for them along the following lines:

> To be true and just in all my dealings, to obey my master and the Golf Club Peon, to keep strict silence on the tee, not to halt nor lag by the wayside through the green and to stand quite still when the Dorai is putting. To keep my hands from stealing golf balls, to clean the clubs lest they grow

rusty, not to wrongly ask for too much salli, and to learn and labour, to get my own living by the honourable estate of Golf Club podian.

If they conducted themselves along these lines they could be paid the fee of twenty-five cents for eighteen holes, including the cleaning of clubs.

The Colombo records also mention the appointment, in 1902, of a flagman to guard the railway level crossing. In 1911 the caddies went on strike again. In 1917, a Mr Denham offered to start a school for caddies; he was willing to pay a teacher and to provide free books. In 1928 the caddies went on strike. In 1947 they formed a union — and immediately went on strike again.

Not all golf in India was played at a Golf Club because many would-be golfers were anything from 600 to 1000 miles from the nearest club. This was not, of course, enough to stop them playing. In 1905 *Golf Monthly* reported the case of a tea planter in Assam. He was many miles from the nearest neighbour and an impossible distance from any golf course. He decided to make his own golf course but did not wish to play entirely by himself, so he taught his Indian house boy to play. He then started his coolie force making a three-hole golf course. With the golf course complete, he and the house boy were going to play on the following day.

During the night there was an earthquake and the course disappeared; his force were set to work to make a further three-hole golf course. When complete, he and the house boy prepared for their first round. Before they could get on the course the tea planter had a massive heart attack and died. His servants buried him behind the third green.

The different conditions in which golf was played meant that there had to be some flexibility in the rules to suit local conditions and this meant variations in the use of caddies. The author once played in central India on

△ *The drive-off, Colombo. The ability* *of small boys to copy a golf swing is clear.*

a golf course composed of rock with sand greens. Each player had a caddie and a forecaddie, the latter was essential, partly because, if the ball hit a rock face, it could ricochet off in any direction and partly because, when it finally came to rest, a kite hawk might swoop down and make off with it. The forecaddie, a sort of mobile scarecrow, was kept pretty busy, leaping ahead and waving his arms to keep the birds off until the player arrived.

THE FAR EAST

Forecaddies were much in evidence in the primitive conditions in which much golf overseas was played. At Bangkok there were many waterways; as a result, the Golf Course had a lot of water hazards. These contained a particularly smelly black primeval ooze and were, in fact, open sewers. Forecaddies would plunge into this and emerge triumphantly with a ball.

▽ *Some members of the Shanghai Golf Club, photographed on the steps of the Clubhouse in 1902. A typical example of the determination of the British to play golf wherever they happened to be. Two Chinese caddies are included in the group.*

▽ *The Caddies'* *Club took a fatherly*
Championship of the *interest in the caddies*
Shanghai Golf Club, *and acted as 'markers'*
1902. The members of *for the competition.*
this (British) Golf

AFRICA

Another type of forecaddie is described by Longhurst, who says that, in the Sudan there is (or was) only one flag and that this flag is carried by a forecaddie who waited with the flag in the hole until the players had reached the green (which was a sand green) and then ran off to the next hole to await the players.

Small black boy caddies used to teach themselves to play by imitation; having very little money, they devised a club from a bent piece of stout wire; the handle was made by bending the wire back on itself for six to eight inches. This thickened end was covered with rubber from the inner tube of an old motor tyre, held on by fine copper wire. With these primitive clubs they learnt to play all the shots played by their masters.

In other parts of the African continent, in the past, it was customary to employ forecaddies whose job it was to go into the forest lining the fairways and fetch balls out. They were assigned to this task because of the danger of poisonous snakes. One golfer described them as splendid chaps who were very skilful and brave. As evidence of their skill he mentioned that they had only lost two last year!

EUROPE

At the turn of the century all golf in Europe was played by golfers from Great Britain, particularly in France where British holidaymakers were playing golf at Pau in 1857 and at Biarritz from about 1883.

The Royal Antwerp Golf Club was founded in 1888 and golf was played at the Hague in 1904.

Golf in the Channel Islands started in 1878, but that really counts as British golf.

Whereas the Scottish Golf Clubs remained staunchly chauvinistic and employed only male caddies, the European clubs had no such inhibitions and girl caddies were (and still are) numerous. Many of the boys and girls who carried clubs on the Continent were as young as eight or ten. Despite their diminutive size, they seemed quite able to manage a full bag of clubs.

The pool of boy caddies at Pau and Biarritz provided a reservoir from which France, in the early part of this

▽ Le caddie Nicois, 1907. The Golf Club de Nice flourished at this time, being well supported by the British in the winter.

century, derived most of the best professionals — and none was better than Arnaud Massy, a caddie from Biarritz who won the Open in 1907, the first European winner. Few, however, of the caddies of that time went on to be the counterpart of the adult professional caddies in Scotland.

One of the problems with the Continental caddies, at least so far as British golfers were concerned, was the fact that most of them spoke no English; many learnt some phrases and words which they had heard their masters use on certain occasions, without ever understanding the real meaning. When Mr Balfour, skilful golfer and eminent politician, playing at Pau at the end of the 19th century, hit a superb brassie shot at one hole, he turned to his little caddie expecting some words of praise, but was greeted with 'Beastly fluke!' and an admiring smile.

On another occasion, a player with a small French girl caddie was playing remarkably badly and continually losing balls in the trees. Eventually, he hit an enormous hook but failed to see where the ball went; he asked the caddie, 'Ou est cet bal?' To which the little girl replied, with a charming

▽ *Golf in Denmark, 1901. A group of golfers and their caddies at the Golf Club on the Isle of Fanö. The golfers are British and their dress is typical of the time; the Danish caddies seem to have their own style of dress. The Amateur Championship of Denmark was played on this course in 1901.*

▷ *Edward VII made an annual pilgrimage to Homberg Spa in Germany to 'take the waters'. He was interested in sport, including golf. 'High Society' followed him to Homberg each year and it became fashionable to be seen on the golf course.*

The greenkeeper is being suitably attentive to Lady Sandhurst. The caddie in the background seems rather depressed – perhaps Lady S is not a very good golfer?!

smile and complete composure, 'Dans la ★★★★★★★ forêt, comme habitude!'

Some caddies indulged in a curious mixture of French and English slang. A friend of mine playing in France was having a sad day of dipping hooks. He and his partner had two French girl caddies. After one such shot, one caddie asked the other, in French, what had happened and got the reply 'C'est un autre Charlie qui plonge!'

Horace Hutchinson, describing golf in Guernsey at the end of the 19th century, says that it was customary for both boy and girl caddies to have a bet on the game. He went on to say that no one has appreciated the difficulties of putting who has not seen a little girl caddie make the sign of the Cross over the line of a putt, in the hope that you will miss it.

In 1932 Henry Cotton became the professional at the Royal Waterloo

Golf Club in Belgium. He played in
many exhibitions and tournaments in
Belgium and found a good caddie
whom he called 'Louis'. Louis was a
very fit young man, who was very
fond of cycling; it seems that, if
Cotton were playing sixty miles or
more from Waterloo, Louis would
cycle to the club and arrive on the first
tee at, say, nine o'clock in the
morning, carry 36 holes and then
cycle back. Eventually there came a
day when Cotton arrived at a
tournament to find that he had no

△ *A match between*
Henry Cotton and
Walter Hagen at the
Waterloo Golf Club,
Belgium, in 1933.
Cotton won by 6 and 5

over 36 holes. Cotton's
caddie, Louis, is in the
white shirt. Clearly his
unfortunate argument
with his mother was
still in the future!

caddie; Louis had been so reliable that Cotton enquired what had gone wrong. He then discovered that Louis, who lived with his mother, had had an argument with her and had killed her with an axe. He was sentenced to life imprisonment. Cotton afterwards said that he could not remember ever having had an argument with Louis on the course – and he felt that this was just as well!

NORTH AMERICA

Of those Golf Clubs that have records, there is no doubt that the first clubs in North America were in Canada. The first was Royal Montreal Golf Club, founded in 1873. Three years later a Golf Club was started in Quebec.

In the records of the Montreal Club there is little mention of caddies in the early days; probably this was because by no means all the players used one and because the caddies were small boys who knew little about the game and only carried in order to earn some extra pocket money. An old caddie of the Club does not recall any great generosity on the part of the players, he was paid twenty cents a round – and no tip.

In 1891 a rise of pay was allowed, ten cents for the first nine holes and fifteen cents for each nine holes after that. This rise was counterbalanced by a stricter requirement: 'Should any

boy refuse to caddie for a third round, such a boy to receive only fifteen cents for the two rounds and his name to be posted in the Clubroom; members being requested not to employ said boy in future.' All caddies had to have badges, 'Which could be positively withdrawn for misconduct.'

In 1885, when there was a smallpox epidemic, no one was allowed to carry without a certificate of vaccination.

There were no caddies who were in the Scottish caddie class because golf was too new a game. In a rapidly developing society, with no unemployment, carrying was for small boys who would take up proper employment as soon as they were big enough.

A similar state of affairs existed in the USA. The renaissance of golf in America in 1888 involved a few small boys acting as caddies. Many of the early golfers did not require caddies. There were no caddie masters. Within a few years of the start of golf at Yonkers in 1888, American 'know how' had devised methods of mass producing clubs; keepers of the green and craftsmen to make clubs were not required. The American professional (often a British professional who had emigrated) was required to teach members how to play, to sell them clubs and play golf.

Teaching was the main requirement; the golf 'bug' had arrived and everybody wanted to learn and they pursued this aim with typical American thoroughness and determination. The caddie was a small boy trying to earn a little pocket money; one gets the impression that, provided he kept quiet during play and watched the ball, he was a good caddie. Teeing up the ball, advising on the right club, and pointing out the line of a putt were skills that he had not acquired and, in any event, the American golfer preferred to do these things for himself, partly out of rugged independence and partly because he had never encountered a professional caddie and was unaware of the benefits that one could confer.

The speed at which golf developed in the US between 1888 and 1900 is difficult to believe: from 12 players in 1888 to 250,000 in 1900. Unhampered by tradition, they developed their own ideas of how golf should be played and, at that stage, boy caddies were unimportant, but useful, and the value of the adult professional caddie unrecognised.

Some of the small boys developed an interest in, and an aptitude for, golf. If they were really good, they turned to professional golf; this only occasionally meant being a club professional, mostly it meant becoming a tournament player. The American golfer admired excellence and was prepared to pay to watch excellent golf; thus was the lucrative tournament circuit in the USA

started. Such was their keenness to learn from the experts that when Vardon played near New York during his US tour in 1906, the New York Stock Exchange closed for the day.

Although many of the professionals on the new tournament circuit were British immigrant professionals, the Americans were learning fast and American caddies with a talent for playing golf were soon on the trail of the prizes. The efforts of two such men are worth considering.

'Chick' Evans

Evans was born in 1890. At the age of ten he started carrying. He says that he knew nothing of golf and was only interested in the pay (fifteen cents a round). Most of his fellow caddies also took no interest in this new game, but did the job for the money; if they ever saved any it was likely to be spent on a baseball bat. It was only in about 1901, when he had broken his leg and was in plaster, that he read about the great golfers and decided to become a golfer.

▷ An advertisement for Pinehurst, NC, c. 1905.
There are now several courses at Pinehurst. Pinehurst No. 2 was laid out in about 1905 by Donald Ross, originally from Dornoch in Scotland. Ross became a famous golf course architect in the USA.
The American concept, in the early 1900s, of a caddie as a small boy who carried clubs for pocket money but did not know (or care) much about the game, is epitomised here.

Delightful Climatic
Conditions and Ideal
Surroundings Have Made

Pinehurst
North Carolina

The Center of Winter
Out-of-Door Life

GOLF | **HUNTING** | **RIDING** | **TENNIS**

No section in America is more generally recognized by public patronage and official recognition as possessing a drier or purer atmosphere during the winter months

COUNTRY CLUB and MODEL DAIRY. GOLF, TENNIS and TRAP SHOOTING; Frequent Tournaments for desirable prizes

Good Auto Roads in a radius of 50 miles

FOUR HOTELS—The Carolina, now open. This house enjoys a reputation for hospitality and excellence of cuisine. The new addition, to be ready in January, add a large number of rooms with bath, also sixteen sleeping porches and three private parlors. Holly Inn, Berkshire and Harvard, open each in January

NO CONSUMPTIVES RECEIVED AT PINEHURST

The one Pullman Service leaves Washington to Pinehurst via Seaboard Air Line. Through Pullman Service from New York to Pinehurst Only one night out from New York, Boston, Cleveland, Pittsburgh and Cincinnati

Send for Illustrated Literature

GENERAL OFFICE, Pinehurst, North Carolina, or Leonard Tufts, Owner, Boston, Mass.

FRANK PRESBREY CO.

When Evans was a caddie his conditions of work seem to have been much as they were in Great Britain. He had a caddie badge, though there does not seem to have been any grading of caddies. Because he was keen to be a good caddie, he began to carry regularly for players who liked him and he got good tips, so he accomplished his own grading.

Evans had many 'wrinkles' concerning the carrying of golf bags, which in those times were not very well balanced. It was his habit to put a heavy club, such as a niblick, head downwards in the bag, to improve the balance. There was one very bad player who had to use his niblick a great deal; in order to get it out more easily, it was put in the right way up and a smooth stone put in the bottom of the bag to maintain the balance.

Evans records that caddies had good tips from players who did well and that, in consequence, some caddies ensured that their players always got a good lie in the rough, and so on. Shades of the past in Scotland! He does not mention any betting on the games, probably because the caddies were not as interested in the game and its outcome as their knowledgeable counterparts in Scotland would have been. When he became very busy carrying Evans said that he was continually using a fine emery paper to clean the clubs and was 'never without a piece'.

Evans became a famous golfer – but remained an amateur. He won the US Amateur and Open Championships in 1911 and many other lesser tournaments as well. He played in Britain and in France; when 'Chick' went to France the French newspapers announced his arrival with the headline, 'Le petit poulet est arrivée!'

Walter Hagen

Hagen first started carrying as a small boy in 1900. He was paid ten cents a round and a nickel tip. From the start he was in it purely for the money. Unlike Chick Evans, who tried many games before he decided that golf was for him, Hagen was immediately attracted to golf and spent all his spare time hitting golf balls. Like Evans, he was determined to be a good caddie, because it meant more money; he learnt, as Evans had, that one way to find a ball in difficult ground was to lie down and roll over the ground until he felt a hard object under him.

At fifteen, Hagen got a job as assistant professional at his local club. From that start he went on to win seventy-five Championships, including the Open four times and the US Open twice and won, in all, one million dollars. Evans said of Hagen that he was in golf to live and not to make a living but his manager said of him, 'Walter sees life through the hole in the doughnut – but he keeps his hand on the dough!'

△ *Walter Hagen, born 1898 in East Rochester, USA. A great golfer,* *he was not a straight driver but his wonderful recovery* *shots out of the deepest rough meant that he scored well and gave* *the spectators an exciting time.*

The heroes in early American golf were the caddies who went on to be famous golfers, both professional and amateur. This tradition has continued, Lee Trevino was a caddie, Byron Nelson was a caddie, Sam Snead was a caddie and there are many others beside. But there remain, in recent years, many who have got to the top who arrived there by a different route. Legislation in the USA does not allow a boy to carry golf clubs until he is over fourteen years of age; as a result the small boy caddie has been eliminated.

College golf

However, a system has existed for many years in the US by which a talented young golfer can attend college on a golf scholarship; a certain academic standard is expected, but the prime requirement is an ability to play golf. As a result, college golf in the United States is of a very high standard and many graduates go on to be top international golfers, first as amateurs and, later, as professionals. Caddie golf is not the only reservoir from which the top American professionals are drawn.

THE TRADITION CONTINUES

Because the American golfers had never had access to really good professional caddies they were unaware of their value. Sarazen, Lema and many other US professionals, when they came to Britain to play found out, for the first time, how much help a professional caddie could be. When Miss Dorothy Campbell, a famous lady golfer from America, visited Britain to play, she remarked on her return how lucky lady golfers in Britain were to have the services of knowledgeable caddies.

Profiting from the experience with professional caddies in the UK, the US professionals, now playing on the US 'tour' for large sums of money, began to require good caddies to help them win the prize money. They were willing to pay handsomely for this expertise (when Gary Player won the US Open he gave all the prize money to his caddie) and thus was created an army of expert caddies who followed the tournaments in the same way, and for the same reasons, that a smaller number did in the UK.

In 1968, George Plimpton, an

▷ 'The Caddy', *from an American golf magazine of 1913. It sums up the attitude of most American players to caddies, an attitude* *which was to change, at least among professionals, when they encountered expert adult caddies in the United Kingdom.*

The Caddy.

A CADDY is a little boy
  No bigger than a minute ;
His heart is always filled with joy—
  His head has nothing in it.
His function is to carry clubs
  When golfers swat the pill ;
He turns good players into dubs
  Because he won't keep still.

You pay him twenty cents an hour,
  To swing your favorite brassie ;
You call him down with all your power :
  He answers pert and sassy.
He is supposed to watch the ball ;
  It's purely supposition ;
He never finds it in the tall ;
  He swipes it, in addition.

It matters not how slow you play,
  He simply can't keep up ;
It seems they all have been this way
  Since Hector was a pup.
You urge him on with gentle mien
  But still he'll loaf and lag,
And when you reach the putting-green
  There's none to hold the flag.

When Peter calls his final "Fore !"
  And all good golfers go
To play the course where every score
  Is bogey or below,
The caddies all will be first class,
  Then we will be in clover ;
We'll lose no balls there in the grass,
  Because – 'twill be burned over.
      From the " American Golfer."

American golf writer, anxious to know what it was really like to play on the circuit, got himself invited to a number of the important 'pro-ams'. In the course of this adventure he learnt something about caddies on the professional circuit.

At his first tournament he arrived rather late. All the better caddies had been booked to carry for the best professionals. The less competent caddies had gone out with the less well known professionals and the better amateurs; the incompetent caddies were for the latecomers. He says that his caddie, Abe, was an elderly sad looking man dressed in several layers of outsize clothes. He had originally been a sailor — a remarkable similarity to the old time casual caddies of Scotland. During the first nine holes, during which Plimpton played quite well, the caddie announced that 'we' were going to have an interesting tournament — a remark that brings him even closer to Scotland; unfortunately, in the course of the second nine holes, during which Plimpton played very badly, it changed to 'you' for all the bad shots.

The age old, and universal, caddie tricks were also in evidence, such as when Abe took ten balls to the practice ground and came away with twenty!

Plimpton records a story of Tommy Bolt, one of the top professionals, whose temper was so unstable that he was prone to a lot of club throwing when things were not going right. Bolt came to a hole and was about 350 yards from the green. The caddie said that the shot was either a No. 2 or a No. 3 iron. Bolt said that that was ridiculous, as he could not have reached the green, even with a driver. The caddie replied that these were the only two clubs left in the bag, unless Bolt wished to use the putter, but pointed out that the putter had no handle, as Bolt had snapped it off in the first nine!

Here, as everywhere, the caddies' conversation, when they all got together, was about golf and the players for whom they caddied. At any tournament there would be about forty tour caddies and a number of local caddies. Most of the caddies travelled to the tournament course in the hope that they would get 'a bag to pack'. In the US they travelled around by car, each car containing as many caddies as could be got into it; they were mostly blacks and travelled with very little luggage, sleeping rough. Many of them had splendid nicknames such as, 'Cut Shot', 'Texas Sam', etc; some of them were the favourite and regular caddie of one of the top professionals, so they were assured of a 'bag to pack'.

These professional caddies were expert at getting the best out of a player and were not frightened to tell him to his face where he was wrong if, by doing so, they could encourage him to relax or, perhaps, concentrate better.

The American caddies were the counterpart of their Scottish fellow caddies, even though they had never met; all they did was to adapt their skills to the conditions of US circuit golf. One caddie, who they much respected, was called Hagan; he it was who first made a scientific study of the golf course and pin positions on each morning for a tournament, so that he could advise his master of exact distances throughout the course.

Despite this, there was a definite division between the top professionals (and among the caddies, also) as to whether a player should depend heavily on his caddie, or should make his own mind up about what clubs to use, lines of putts, and so on. There was, however, no division among the US professionals who had played in Britain about the need for an expert caddie there. Gary Brewer, one of the US professionals who played in the UK in the 1960s, spoke of the incredible self confidence and expertise of the British caddie. He pointed out that the wind on the British seaside courses meant that markers were useless, a modest change of wind strength and direction could mean a difference of four clubs, or more, for a shot of the same length, between one day and the next.

The old tradition of the Scottish professional caddie still exists in many parts of the world but the originators of that tradition are acknowledged as the best.

7. WOMEN CADDIES

△ *The French Ladies' Championship at Le Touquet Golf Club, 1913. The golfer has played out of some rushes; she wears gloves, not for the reason that golfers of today wear them but in order to prevent her hands getting calloused. The French caddie is a woman and wears a pinafore, but no hat.*

Traditionally, caddies were boys or men and in that part of the British Isles where golf is a tradition, namely Scotland, women and girl caddies are not to be found, although, in about 1870, there was a hiccup, when the caddies at Gullane went on strike. During the strike, girl caddies were employed; this went on for six weeks until the shame was too much for the boys and they went back to work. It is also said, by Sheridan, who was born and brought up at North Berwick and became Caddie Master at Sunningdale, that the girls from Dirleton village used to carry at the Archerfield Golf Club, near

▷ *Lytham and St Annes Golf Club, 1890. A group, which includes one girl caddy, outside the professional's shop. Lytham was one of the first Golf Clubs in Britain to allow girls to carry. At the 1897 Meeting girl caddies outnumbered the boys. The girl caddie in this picture wears a 'Tam o' Shanter' and a white pinafore — exactly the same as that worn by her sister caddies in Guernsey (page 117).*

Gullane. Nevertheless, the Scottish tradition remains that boys and men are caddies, women and girls are not.

When golf spread to England, the tradition, carried by the Scots, was maintained but, when the golf explosion came, the tradition weakened slightly.

The Royal Liverpool Golf Club at Hoylake makes no mention of women and girl caddies in its history, nor were they ever part of the scene at Royal Blackheath but the Royal Lytham and St Annes Golf Club, founded in 1886, had no inhibitions and girl caddies were employed from about 1890. At first they were only allowed to carry for lady members and only girls over fourteen were permitted to carry. By 1897 they were carrying for the men as well and in the Autumn Meeting of that year there were more girl than boy caddies. There was an annual Christmas party, and capes were issued to caddies on wet days.

The girls soon learnt to be tough; there was one very large and bad tempered member who had been known, when in a rage, to pick up his caddie and shake him 'like a rabbit' and had thrown a caddie over a boundary fence when the latter refused to climb over to fetch a ball. When this member arrived at the Club, the caddies used to hide so as not to have to carry for him. He got his come uppance from a thirteen-year-old girl caddie; he hit his ball on

to a railway line and was so infuriated that he threw the club away, whereupon his girl caddie said, 'You can go and find your own b****y ball, and carry your own clubs, too!' She then threw down the clubs and walked back to the Clubhouse. On the next occasion that he played golf the man particularly asked for her to carry for him.

AUNT POLLY

Just after the turn of the century, Royal Ashdown Golf Club employed a remarkable woman as a caddie. It seems that she was, in all probability, the only female caddie at the Club. Her name was Mrs Mitchell but she seems to have been universally known as 'Aunt Polly'. She was one of the

△ The 1913 Ladies' Championship at Lytham and St Annes. As Fanny Brooks, one of the Club's girl caddies, makes a tee, the competitor seems to be waggling a club rather too close to her.

great family of Mitchells who had a long association with the Club and with its Artisan Club; one of the better known Mitchells was Abe Mitchell, who became a great professional golfer.

Aunt Polly did not start as a girl caddie, but when she was a married woman with a small child. Her husband worked on the course. The reason we know a lot about Mrs Mitchell is that she kept a private journal of the various happenings of her life as a caddie, and it is quite clear that she took to carrying as a duck to water.

She and her husband lived in a cottage that was very close to the professional's shop; because she was so near, the professional would ask her to carry when he was short of caddies. Her little boy was then two and a half years old. On one occasion when the professional asked her to carry she told him that she did not know what to do with her little boy and the professional said that she could leave him in the shop and that he would look after him. When she came back, the little boy was playing with some pieces of old golf shafts and some pitch! After a lot of work she got the child clean but decided not to use the professional's shop as a nursery thereafter!

Aunt Polly said that she enjoyed carrying but did not like making sand tees and was very glad when the little

△ Newquay, 1901. Daughters of local fishermen earned money for the family by carrying clubs.

peg tees appeared. Once her children were at school she was able to carry two rounds a day.

On one occasion she carried for the Bishop of London when he played in a match against a younger clergyman. She says, 'I did my best to help him (it was a scorching hot day) but the other gentleman was too good for us [note the 'us'] the Bishop felt the heat, as he was dressed in thick tweeds.'

On another occasion her gentleman put a ball into a hollow full of long grass, when he played, two balls came out. 'Then we had to make sure that we had played the right ball.' Once she carried for a gentleman who was a Peer of the Realm, no less. It was pouring with rain and her gentleman was playing very badly. Aunt Polly kept looking at him because she thought something was wrong, but could not decide what it was. Then she realised, and asked him to put his hand in his pocket — he could not — and she pointed out that he had his mackintosh trousers on the wrong way round. 'So he took them off and I put them in the bag. After that he played quite well.'

She always had a tiny bag with her in which she kept: a sponge (for cleaning the ball), score card, pencil, penknife, matches, golf tees (after wooden tee pegs came in), soft rag to wipe the clubs, emery paper, and a clean handkerchief.

She carried for a Major Devitt, 'he had only a thin pair of shoes, no nails, no rubbers, and he kept slipping. So he took off his shoes and played the 16th and 17th in his socks. But the gorse made him dance around when his ball went in to it, which happened

△ *A Ladies' Golf Tournament at Portrush, Northern Ireland, 1913. Two girl caddies carry for the players, whose costumes suggest that ankles are now permitted!*

116

fairly often.'

Aunt Polly was a real caddie — and a great character — and it is fortunate for us that she wrote an account of her life on the course.

There was an 'Aunt Polly' at Westward Ho!, the redoubtable Mrs Williams who was a First Class caddie in 1910 (see page 44).

A TEMPORARY MEASURE

Sunningdale Golf Club, with Sheridan as Caddie Master and plenty of rich members, had no difficulty in keeping a nucleus of good professional caddies. Sheridan did a lot to teach the young caddies and frequently helped caddies over difficult times. Girl caddies were unnecessary — until the First World War. It was at this time that Sheridan bethought himself of the lasses of Dirleton who, in his youth at North Berwick, had carried at Archerfield. He had girl caddies at Sunningdale during the War, but, true to his Scottish traditions, did not employ them once the War was over.

GUERNSEY

Guernsey — but not, it seems, its sister Jersey — had girl caddies in 1890, although they may have been carrying before that: Royal Lytham and St Annes voiced their opinion that Guernsey was the first area where women caddies were employed. The

▽ *The small stool seems more suitable for the girl caddie than her master; cartoon, 1911.*

△ *Girl caddies in Guernsey, 1901. The white pinafore and the 'Tam o' Shanter' bonnet was a uniform* *that they all wore. Visitors said that they were very hardy, very keen and very knowledgeable caddies.*

bare-headed and bare-legged girls of Guernsey caddied from an early age and all golfers who went there were impressed by their cheerfulness and competence.

FRANCE

In France, in particular, girl caddies have always been accepted. Their problems with the English language

△ *The French Ladies'*
Championship at Le
Touquet, 1913. The
girl caddie is laden
down with extra
clothes, as well as a
golf bag. The player is
British, as were nearly
all the competitors.
The pine trees and
sand are typical of Le
Touquet Golf Course.

have already been mentioned. As an
example of willingness, but not of
expertise, a tale is told of a golfer,
with a girl caddie, who put his ball
into some very deep rough. After a
prolonged search without success, the
golfer gave up and called to the girl to
leave the search and go on to the next
tee. He walked on but soon became
aware that she was not following but
was still searching the rough. He
called her to hurry up and added that
the ball could be left. It then transpired
that she was looking for the clubs!

THE USA

In the USA, women and girls as
caddies have never been popular, the
following story seems to underline
this. On 3 June 1904, the *Chicago
Sunday Herald* reported:

Mr John D. Rockefeller has 10-12
girl caddies to choose from. As far
as we know he is the only golfer in
the world who uses girl caddies. He
is subjected to much annoyance by
the chagrined youths who view this
departure with alarm, 'Petticoats!
Petticoats! Cheap labour!' they yell.
It is said that Mr Rockefeller does
not employ the girls because they
work for half the price of the boys,
but because he finds the lasses more
willing in going over the course.
He is a very slow player, and the
boy caddies who like to follow
quick, clean play, used to loll on

△ *Golf at The Hague
Golf Club, September
1913. The players
wear jackets and white
flannel trousers and the
girl caddies wear a
uniform of white
pinafore and broad-*
*brimmed straw hat.
The tee box is of a type
that is still seen on
some of our older
courses, but now
contains wrappers from
golf balls and used
drink cans.*

the grass and almost fall asleep, instead of following on his heels as a good caddie should.

In 1901, three years earlier, the Mayswood Golf Club, Illinois, reported that girl caddies — daughters of members of the Club — had been employed at fifteen cents a round,'but', the account went on 'it is doubtful if the experiment will be continued'.

In all, it seems that, except for France and Guernsey, caddies are, and always were, predominantly male. Whether, if caddie carts and buggies had not been invented, the large numbers of golfers requiring help would have resulted in girl caddies being widely used, we shall never know.

8. CADDIES OF ANOTHER SORT

Not all caddies were human. In the late 1800s the Earl of Wemyss was a keen and skilful golfer. He was a man of very decided opinions and resigned from the Wimbledon Golf Club because he was asked to wear a red coat when playing. He also had strong views on the cutting up of golf courses by iron clubs, and had a set of wooden clubs made for him with which he played all shots. At the age of 96 he was still playing; as the walks between shots were tiring, he used a chestnut cob to carry him.

General Sir John Low of Clatto was Captain of the R & A in 1865. He, too, was still playing golf when he was over 90. He commonly rode a pony to help him around the course.

In his later years as professional to the Penina Golf Club in Portugal, Henry Cotton used a donkey to carry his clubs.

Finally, a different form of carrying. In 1902, the British Amateur Championship was played at Hoylake. C. K. Hutchings played S. H. Fry in the Final. Hutchings was a local player and not in the first flush of youth; he had had a long haul getting to the Final and it was recognised that he was tired. When he went in to lunch at the end of the first round, he was eight up. His friends thought that, as he was clearly going to win well out 'in the country', it would be a nice gesture to take a chair out in the afternoon, so that they could 'chair' him back to the Clubhouse after his victory. After lunch his opponent staged a remarkable recovery, and won six holes. In the event, Hutchings had to hole a good putt on the last green to win — which he did. The perspiring and tired carriers of the chair had now carried it for eighteen holes in order to carry the winner two hundred yards to the Clubhouse!

◁ *A painting by Thomas Hodge, c. 1870, of General Sir John Low of Clatto (near St Andrews) riding up the 18th fairway on his cream pony. Low was a much loved and revered member of the Royal and Ancient Golf Club, of which he was Captain in 1865. He lived to a ripe old age and was still playing when he was over 80. When walking became tedious, he used to ride his pony, dismounting to play each shot.*

BIBLIOGRAPHY

GOLF CLUBS

St Andrews: Home of Golf
J. K. Robertson, St Andrews, 1967

The Story of the R & A
J. B. Salmond, London, 1956

Archives of Prestwick Golf Club

Prestwick St Nicholas Golf Club
William Galbraith, Prestwick, 1950

Prestwick Golf Club
James E. Shaw, Glasgow, 1938

The Golf Book of East Lothian
John Kerr, Edinburgh, 1896

The Golf House Club, Elie
Alastair M. Drysdale, Elie, 1975

The Lytham Century
E. A. Nickson, Lytham St Annes,
1982

*The Royal Liverpool Golf Club:
A History, 1869-1932*
Guy B. Farrar, Birkenhead, 1933

The History of Littlestone Golf Club
Littlestone, Sussex, 1988

*The History of Royal Wimbledon
Golf Club*
C. Cruikshank, London, 1986

*Walton Heath Golf Club: The Story
of the First Seventy-Five Years*
C. Hewertson, London, 1979

Royal Calcutta Golf Club, 1829-1979
Pearson Surita, Calcutta, 1979

*Royal Colombo Golf Club: 100 Years,
1879-1979*
Fernando, Kadirgamar & Caudappa,
Colombo, 1979

*The Royal Montreal Golf Club,
1873-1973*
Duncan C. Campbell, Montreal, 1973

The Bobby Jones Story
O. B. Keeler,
reprint, The Old Golf Shop Inc,
Cincinnati, 1980

Golf is my Game
Bobby Jones, London, 1948

The Byron Nelson Story
Morton W. Olman, Cincinnati, 1980

Chick Evans' Golf Book
Charles 'Chick' Evans, Chicago, 1921

The Walter Hagen Story
Walter Hagen, London, 1957

This Game of Golf
H. Cotton, London, 1948

'Green Memories'
Bernard Darwin, London, 1928

Taylor on Golf
J. H. Taylor, London, 1902

Fifty Years of Golf: My Memories
Andrew Kirkaldy, London, 1921

Fifty Years of Golf
Horace G. Hutchinson, London, 1914

Life of Tom Morris
W. W. Tulloch, London, 1908

Golf: My Life's Work
J. H. Taylor, London, 1943

Sheridan of Sunningdale
J. Sheridan, London, 1967

Mrs Mitchell's Recollections
Original MS by kind permission of
Mr Robert Mitchell

GENERAL BOOKS ON GOLF

Early Golf at Edinburgh and Leith
David Hamilton, Glasgow, 1988

The Art of Golf
Sir W. G. Simpson, Edinburgh, 1892

Golf: The Badminton Library
Horace G. Hutchinson and others,
London, 1914

In the Wind's Eye
Alistair Beatson Adamson,
Edinburgh, 1980

Only on Sundays
H. Longhurst, London, 1964

Sixty Years of Golf
Robert Harris, London, 1953

Golf in the Making
I. Henderson and D. Stirk,
Winchester, 1978

Golf
Bernard Darwin, London, 1954

Great Golfers in the Making
Henry Leach, Edinburgh, 1907

The Story of American Golf
Herbert Warren Wind, New York,
1948

The Golfer's Handbook, 1912

Golf, Arnaud Massy, London 1927

The Bogey Man
George Plimpton, London, 1969

Encyclopaedia of Golf
Webster Evans, London, 1971

Down the Nineteenth Fairway
P. Dobereiner, Glasgow, 1982

GENERAL REFERENCE BOOKS

The Thoughts of Thomas Kincaid
1687-88
National Library, Advocates,
Manuscript 32/7/7

The Account Books of Sir Thomas Foulis
1672-1707
Scottish Historical Society Extracts,
1894

An Etymological Dictionary of the
Scottish Language
John Jamieson DD, FRSE, FSAS
Second edition, Edinburgh, 1840

Dr John Jamieson's Scottish Dictionary
& Supplement
Edinburgh, 1841

Chambers Etymological Dictionary of the
English Language
W. & R. Chambers, London &
Edinburgh, 1885

MAGAZINES

The *Field* Magazine, various volumes
1860-1880
F. P. Hopkins, London

Golf Monthly

Golf Illustrated 1899-1929

Acknowledgements

I have received kind help and sound advice from a host of people, too numerous to mention, to all of whom I extend grateful thanks. Specifically, I thank the following:

Mr R. A. L. Burnet, Archivist and Librarian of the Royal and Ancient Golf Club of St Andrews, for his help in the research, in which he demonstrated both his great knowledge of the history of golf and his patience.

Mr D. C. Smail of the Prestwick Golf Club, editor of the newly published and highly successful *Prestwick Golf Club: The Birthplace of the Open,* for all his help in finding material in the Prestwick Golf Club Archives relating to caddies.

The Royal and Ancient Golf Club, for permission to reproduce pictures of four St Andrews' caddies on pages 41, 67, 70 and 71.

Prestwick Golf Club, for permission to reproduce the photograph on the back dust jacket, a group of caddies on page 14 and the picture of General Sir Hope Grant and caddie on page 16.

Royal Blackheath Golf Club, for permission to reproduce the pictures of Corporal Sharpe and Old Alick on pages 9 and 10.

The Royal North Devon Golf Club, for permission to reproduce the picture of a group of young caddies on pages 12 and 13.

The Royal Burgess Golfing Society of Edinburgh, for permission to reproduce the picture of Daft Willie Gunn on page 6.

Mr Angus Lloyd of the Burlington Galleries, London, for permission to reproduce the picture of the caddie on the front dust cover, the picture of Dr Laidlaw Purves at Wimbledon on the title page and the picture 'Stymied' on pages 32-33.

Littlestone Golf Club, for permission to reproduce pictures of the caddie badge on page 50 and the lunch and tea tokens on page 49.

Mr E. A. Nickson, author of *The Lytham Century*, for permission to reproduce the pictures of caddies at Lytham on pages 48 and 113.

Country Life Ltd, for permission to reproduce two pictures of Henry Cotton and caddie on pages 85 and 102.

Sean Arnold of Sean Arnold Ltd of Berlin and London, for permission to reproduce the picture of the Pinehurst caddie on page 105.

I am grateful to H. Pattisson & Co Ltd of Luton for permission to use the extracts from their catalogue of 1910 on pages 27, 35, 58 and 79.

Last, but not least, it is a pleasure to thank Mr Philip Truett, Museum Curator of Walton Heath Golf Club, for his unfailing kindness, help and patience.